ARIZONA

The
CREAKY KNEES
Guide

THE **80** BEST EASY HIKES

ARIZONA

The
CREAKY KNEES
Guide

THE 80 BEST EASY HIKES

Bruce Grubbs

SASQUATCH BOOKS
SEATTLE

Printed in the United States of America

Published by Sasquatch Books
17 16 15 14 13 12   9 8 7 6 5 4 3 2 1

Cover photograph: © Ocean Photography / Veer
Cover design: Sarah Plein
Interior design: Rosebud Eustace
Interior photographs and maps: Bruce Grubbs
Interior composition: Sarah Plein

Library of Congress Cataloging-in-Publication Data is available.

ISBN-13: 978-1-57061-812-3

Important Note: Please use common sense. No guidebook can act as a substitute for experience, careful planning, the right equipment, and appropriate training. There is inherent
danger in all the activities described in this book, and readers must assume full respon-
sibility for their own actions and safety. Changing or unfavorable conditions in weather,
roads, trails, snow, waterways, and so forth cannot be anticipated by the author or publisher, but should be considered by any outdoor participants. The author and publisher will
not be responsible for the safety of users of this guide.

Sasquatch Books
1904 Third Avenue, Suite 710
Seattle, WA 98101
(206) 467-4300
www.sasquatchbooks.com
custserv@sasquatchbooks.com

SUSTAINABLE FORESTRY INITIATIVE
Label applies to the text stock

Certified Sourcing
www.sfiprogram.org
SFI-00341

Contents

Big Lake in the White Mountains—part of the stunning variety to be found in Arizona's backcountry, which encompasses alpine mountains, meadows, and forests, as well as rugged desert.

CONTENTS

Hikes at a Glance

Stroll in the Park

NO.	HIKE NAME	RATING	BEST SEASON	KIDS	DOGS
10	Wupatki Ruin	🚶🚶🚶🚶	Year-round	✔	
61	Signal Hill Trail	🚶🚶🚶	Fall–spring	✔	

Easy Walk

NO.	HIKE NAME	RATING	BEST SEASON	KIDS	DOGS
4	Rim Trail	🚶🚶🚶🚶🚶	Year-round	✔	
13	Kendrick Park Watchable Wildlife Trail	🚶🚶🚶	Summer, fall	✔	
20	Mormon Lake	🚶🚶🚶	Spring–fall	✔	✔
26	Bear Sign Canyon	🚶🚶🚶🚶	Spring, fall	✔	✔
28	West Fork Trail	🚶🚶🚶🚶	Spring–fall	✔	
31	Huckaby Trail	🚶🚶🚶🚶	Year-round	✔	✔
33	Bell Trail	🚶🚶🚶🚶🚶	Spring–fall	✔	✔
36	Kinder Crossing Trail	🚶🚶🚶🚶	Spring–fall	✔	✔
38	Tunnel Trail	🚶🚶🚶	Summer, fall	✔	✔
54	Go John Trail	🚶🚶🚶🚶	Fall–spring	✔	✔
67	Sugarloaf Mountain	🚶🚶🚶🚶	Year-round	✔	
68	Echo Canyon	🚶🚶🚶🚶🚶	Year-round	✔	
70	Buena Vista Peak	🚶🚶🚶🚶	Spring–fall	✔	✔
72	Rucker Canyon	🚶🚶🚶🚶	Spring–fall	✔	✔
79	Palm Canyon	🚶🚶🚶	Fall–spring	✔	

Moderate Workout

NO.	HIKE NAME	RATING	BEST SEASON	KIDS	DOGS
2	Ken Patrick Trail	🚶🚶🚶🚶🚶	Summer, fall		
9	White House Ruin Trail	🚶🚶🚶🚶	Spring–fall	✔	
18	Sunset-Brookbank Loop	🚶🚶🚶🚶	Summer, fall		✔
21	Sycamore Rim Trail	🚶🚶🚶	Summer, fall		✔
22	Kelsey-Dorsey Loop	🚶🚶🚶🚶	Summer, fall		✔
23	Secret Mountain Trail	🚶🚶🚶🚶	Summer, fall		✔
24	Loy Canyon Trail	🚶🚶🚶🚶	Fall–spring		✔
25	Secret Canyon	🚶🚶🚶🚶🚶	Spring, fall		✔
27	Thomas Point Trail	🚶🚶🚶🚶	Spring–fall	✔	✔

No.	Hike Name	Rating	Best Season	Kids	Dogs
29	AB Young Trail	🚶🚶🚶🚶	Spring–fall		✔
32	Munds Mountain Trail	🚶🚶🚶🚶	Spring–fall		✔
34	West Clear Creek	🚶🚶🚶🚶🚶	Spring–fall		✔
35	Fossil Springs Trail	🚶🚶🚶🚶	Spring–fall		✔
39	Horton Creek	🚶🚶🚶🚶	Summer, fall	✔	✔
40	Woodchute Trail	🚶🚶🚶	Summer, fall		✔
41	Granite Mountain Trail	🚶🚶🚶🚶	Spring–fall		✔
45	Barks Canyon	🚶🚶🚶🚶	Fall–spring		✔
49	Apache Railroad Trail	🚶🚶🚶🚶	Summer, fall		✔
55	Pass Mountain Trail	🚶🚶🚶🚶	Fall–spring		✔
56	Margies Cove Trail	🚶🚶🚶🚶	Fall–spring		✔
57	Table Top Trail	🚶🚶🚶🚶	Fall–spring		✔
58	Wilderness of Rocks	🚶🚶🚶🚶	Summer, fall		✔
64	Aravaipa Canyon	🚶🚶🚶🚶🚶	Spring–fall		
71	Chiricahua Peak	🚶🚶🚶🚶🚶	Summer, fall		✔
74	Sycamore Creek	🚶🚶🚶🚶	Spring, fall		✔
75	Cherum Peak Trail	🚶🚶🚶	Spring, fall		✔
77	Vulture Peak	🚶🚶🚶🚶	Fall–spring		✔
78	Ben Avery Trail	🚶🚶🚶🚶	Fall–spring		✔
80	Bull Pasture	🚶🚶🚶🚶	Fall–spring		

Prepare to Perspire

No.	Hike Name	Rating	Best Season	Kids	Dogs
3	Nankoweap/Saddle Mountain Trail	🚶🚶🚶🚶	Spring–fall		✔
8	Paria Canyon	🚶🚶🚶🚶🚶	April, May, October		✔
11	Bill Williams Mountain Trail	🚶🚶🚶🚶	Summer, fall		✔
12	Kendrick Peak Trail	🚶🚶🚶🚶	Summer, fall		✔
14	Aubineau–Bear Jaw Canyon Loop	🚶🚶🚶🚶	Summer, fall		✔
15	Humphreys Peak Trail	🚶🚶🚶🚶	Summer, fall		✔
16	Kachina Trail	🚶🚶🚶🚶🚶	Summer, fall		✔
17	Inner Basin Trail	🚶🚶🚶🚶🚶	Summer, fall		✔
19	Walnut Canyon Rim	🚶🚶🚶	Summer, fall		✔
30	Wilson Mountain Trail	🚶🚶🚶🚶	Spring–fall		✔
37	Cabin Loop	🚶🚶🚶🚶	Summer, fall		✔
42	Pine Mountain	🚶🚶🚶🚶	Spring–fall		✔
43	Y Bar Basin–Barnhardt Canyon Loop	🚶🚶🚶🚶🚶	Spring–fall		✔
44	Browns Peak	🚶🚶🚶🚶	Spring–fall		✔

46	Dutchmans Loop	🚶🚶🚶🚶	Fall–spring		✔
47	Fireline Loop	🚶🚶🚶🚶	Spring, fall		✔
48	Escudilla Mountain	🚶🚶🚶🚶	Summer, fall		✔
50	West Baldy Trail	🚶🚶🚶🚶🚶	Summer, fall		✔
51	East Baldy Trail	🚶🚶🚶🚶🚶	Summer, fall		✔
52	KP Creek	🚶🚶🚶🚶	Summer, fall		✔
53	Bear Wallow Trail	🚶🚶🚶🚶	Summer, fall		✔
62	Hugh Norris Trail	🚶🚶🚶🚶🚶	Fall–spring		
63	King Canyon Trail	🚶🚶🚶🚶	Fall–spring		
65	Powers Garden	🚶🚶🚶🚶	Spring, fall		✔
66	Cochise Stronghold East	🚶🚶🚶🚶	Year-round		✔
69	Heart of Rocks	🚶🚶🚶🚶🚶	Spring, fall		
76	Wabayuma Peak	🚶🚶🚶	Spring–fall		✔

Knee-Punishing

NO.	HIKE NAME	RATING	BEST SEASON	KIDS	DOGS
1	North Canyon Loop	🚶🚶🚶🚶	Summer, fall		✔
5	Boucher–Hermit Loop	🚶🚶🚶🚶🚶	Fall–spring		
6	South Kaibab–Bright Angel Trails	🚶🚶🚶🚶🚶	Fall–spring		
7	Horseshoe Mesa	🚶🚶🚶🚶🚶	Spring, fall		
59	Finger Rock Trail	🚶🚶🚶🚶🚶	Spring, fall		✔
60	Mica Mountain	🚶🚶🚶🚶🚶	Spring		
73	Mount Wrightson	🚶🚶🚶🚶🚶	Summer, fall		✔

Acknowledgments

I wish to thank all of my many hiking companions over the years for putting up with my incessant photography and trail mapping. Thanks also to the agency personnel who have provided me with up-to-date information over more than thirty years of writing Arizona guidebooks—you are now too numerous to mention. Thank you to all the trail volunteers who work so hard to keep Arizona's trails open. And warm thanks to Duart Martin, who has aided and abetted yet another book project. Finally, thank you to Gary Luke, Rachelle Longé, Liza Brice-Dahmen, Nancy Cortelyou, Shari Miranda, Sarah Plein, Christy Cox, and all the fine people at Sasquatch Books for turning my rough scribblings into a finished book.

Introduction

Arizona—a land of windblown sand, weird-looking cactus, and scorching temperatures, right? Well, yes, I'll admit it does have those. But it also has vast forested plateaus, towering mountains reaching above timberline, shimmering lakes nestled in alpine meadows, red sandstone monoliths rising starkly out of the desert floor, hidden streams winding through secret canyons, and isolated mountain ranges adrift in a sea of desert.

Geographically, the state is divided into two provinces by the Mogollon Rim (pronounced "mug-e-on"), a generally south-facing, 2,000-foot line of bluffs and cliffs. To the south and west of the Mogollon Rim lies the basin and range country, which consists of isolated mountain ranges separated by broad valleys. The Colorado Plateau stretches north of the rim—a vast, high-elevation tableland cut by thousands of canyons and punctuated by lofty volcanic mountains.

The basin and range country varies in character, from long, low desert mountains separated by 10- to 40-mile-wide desert plains in the southwest and west, to the "sky island" ranges of southeastern Arizona, which form forested islands rising 5,000 feet above the surrounding grasslands. In central Arizona, the ranges are more rugged and the valleys narrower.

Understanding the great elevation range, from 70 feet to 12,633 feet, and the effect of the seasons is key to enjoying the outdoors in Arizona. While the summer heat is truly appalling in the desert (the record high temperature is 128 degrees F and June temperatures in the 110-plus range are common), meanwhile, the mountains of northern and eastern Arizona and the tops of the sky island ranges in the southeast are moderate, with temperatures in the 70s and 80s. And the time to engage in canyoneering—exploring deep, narrow canyons—is when warm weather makes getting wet fun instead of a chilly ordeal.

At the other extreme, winter low temperatures in the mountains have plunged as low as -40 degrees F. But when the high country is blanketed in snow, the southern deserts are enjoying moderate temperatures. As a bonus, the occasional winter rainstorms start bringing out desert flowers as early as January. By March, if conditions have been favorable, the desert plains and mountain slopes can be awash in color, and creeks that are normally dry are running. Winter storms usually last a couple of days and are followed by days or even weeks of clear, dry weather.

Fall is an absolute delight everywhere in Arizona. The summer heat has moderated, fall color is appearing in the mountains, and the weather is usually dry and stable. Spring hikers enjoy similar weather, except that the northern part of the state occasionally gets strong windstorms.

This book contains a selection of the best hikes in Arizona, which are sometimes the easiest but not always. Keep in mind that even the longer hikes can be made easier simply by turning back sooner. Also, so that I could include a cross section of hikes through the state and not ignore such gems as the Grand Canyon or the Santa Catalina Front Range, I included hikes in such areas even though the hiking is not easy by the very nature of the terrain. And one hiker's strenuous hike is another hiker's easy hike. In order to provide a cross section of the best day hikes and backpack trips in the state, I have included a wide variety of hikes, from 0.25-mile strolls on paved trails to multiday backpack trips in remote canyons and mountains. Just pick the place and the hike that suits you. And remember, the point is to have fun!

Using This Guide

The hikes featured in this book are described approximately north to south and grouped by major geographic areas of the state. At the start of each hike description you'll find a summary to help you decide if the hike is one that suits the needs of you and your party. Each hike includes the following:

TRAIL NUMBER AND NAME

Each trail has a number, which is referred to in the Hikes at a Glance section as well as at the start of each hike description. Official trail names are used whenever possible. When hikes use parts of several trails, the hike is usually named for the main trail. In some cases the hike is named for a major geographic feature, especially in the case of a cross-country hike.

OVERALL RATING

Hikes are rated from one to five, with five being the cream of the crop. But that doesn't mean hikes rated one are awful—there are no awful hikes in this book! It's just that five-rated hikes have everything—good trails or easy walking, spectacular scenery, and no crowds (at least part of the time). Hikes that receive lower ratings may be overcrowded, more difficult to follow, have some sections that are less scenic, and so forth. Be warned—this rating is totally subjective; my one-rated hike may be your five-rated favorite.

DISTANCE

The distance quoted is round-trip for out-and-back hikes along the same trail or loop hikes. A few hikes are best done with a car shuttle, in which case the mileage is described as one-way with a shuttle. Most hikers prefer to spend time hiking rather than doing car shuttles, so I avoid shuttle hikes as much as possible. Some hikes are so fine that it's worth doing a shuttle.

Distances were carefully measured using terrain profiling on digital topographic maps, which makes the mileages consistent throughout the book. My tests have shown that this method is within a few percent of measurements taken with a calibrated trail wheel or bicycle cyclometer. My distances may not agree with official agency distances, which are measured with several different methods and by different people. I've found too many errors in official trail mileages to be willing to use them in this book.

One caution: You can't measure trail distances accurately during your hike with a civilian Global Positioning System receiver. That's because the GPS measures the distance between position fixes every second or so. Since civilian GPS position fixes are guaranteed accurate to 10 meters, at walking speeds they are not accurate enough to measure distance. At higher speeds, the error averages out. The best way to measure trail distance with a civilian GPS is to record a GPS track as you hike and then download it to digital topo maps after the hike. You can then plot a trail profile on which you can measure distances accurately. The reason this works is that the track log points are averaged out in the GPS receiver.

HIKING TIME

The time listed is estimated using the tried-and-true formula that allows for an average speed of 2 miles per hour plus 30 minutes for every 1,000-foot elevation gain or loss. This works out to err on the conservative side compared to the average time that most reasonably fit hikers will take. Practiced, fit hikers will usually be able to go faster, but less fit people or those carrying heavy loads are going to take longer.

Some of the longer day hikes are best done as overnight backpack trips, in which case the time in hours as well as days is listed. There are a few hikes in this book that are multiday backpack trips, pure and simple. That doesn't automatically mean they are death marches! There are some great backpack trips in this state that are fine for beginners.

ELEVATION GAIN

This is an approximation of the total elevation gain or loss on the hike, not including minor ups and downs.

HIGH POINT

The high point of the hike may be the trailhead, since many hikes in Arizona descend canyons. So don't assume you'll be hiking uphill on the way out and downhill on the way back!

EFFORT

Another highly subjective rating—I have friends who regard a 10-day, arduous, cross-country Grand Canyon hike as a stroll in the park. Others regard a mile on a level trail as an astronomical distance requiring superhuman ability. Most hikers fall somewhere in between these extremes, and therefore I have the following ratings for the effort required to do each hike.

A **Stroll in the Park** rating represents short walks of 2 or 3 miles with little elevation change that stick with good trails. Families with small children and those who don't think of themselves as hikers should be able to do these walks.

On a hike rated as an **Easy Walk**, you will find similar conditions to "Stroll in the Park" hikes but with a bit longer distances—up to 5 miles—and with up to about 500 feet of elevation change. Non-hikers can do these if they take it easy.

Now we're getting into hiker treks. Hikes noted as a **Moderate Workout** generally have more than 500 feet of elevation change and up to 5 miles distance round-trip.

Expect **Prepare to Perspire** hikes to have sustained climbs, often of 1,000 feet elevation gain or more, serious ups and downs, and possibly some cross-country hiking. Total distance is usually more than 5 miles and may be much more. You'll get a workout on one of these hikes!

Knee-Punishing hikes involve thousands of feet of ascent or, worse, descent, often on rough, rocky, or faint trails. They also may require cross-country hiking and some rock scrambling. If you're an experienced and fit Arizona hiker, you'll feel thrashed but happy after one of these! If you're a beginner, stay away and learn the ropes on easier hikes. Beginners include experienced hikers who are not familiar with desert hiking, which, because of low humidity, heat, and lack of trailside water sources, is very different from hiking in forests and mountains.

BEST SEASON

Arizona hiking seasons are different from those of more temperate climates. You'll want to stay away from low-elevation desert hikes in the summer, unless you like hiking in a 115-degree blast furnace! On the other hand, desert hikes are very enjoyable in mid-winter when the high country is snow covered, and short desert hikes can be done early in the morning during the summer. In this section I list the best seasons for the hike, but that doesn't mean you can't go at other times.

WATER

If there are any, this section lists known water sources along the route or easily accessible from the trail. While day hikers should carry all the water they need, knowledge of water sources may be important in an emergency. Backpackers must plan their trip around reliable water sources. Note that Arizona state law prohibits camping within 0.25 mile of any spring or isolated water source in order to avoid interference with wildlife, who depend on these sources and may be scared off if you camp too close.

PERMITS/CONTACT
This section lists the contact information for the agency managing the land. If a permit or reservation is required, it will be noted here. Most Arizona trails do not require permits and many don't require fees—but this can change, so it is always good to contact the managing agency or check their website.

MAPS
This section lists the U.S. Geological Survey 7.5-minute topographic maps that cover the hike. Note that not all trails are shown on these maps, but the terrain and natural features are shown very accurately. Some areas are covered by recreational maps that may not show the terrain as well as the USGS maps but do show the trails more accurately; these are listed if available.

NOTES
This section includes such things as whether leashed pets are allowed and other trail users you may encounter such as all-terrain vehicles, mountain bikes, or horses, as well as special considerations unique to this hike.

THE HIKE
This is a brief description of the character of the hike, including whether it's a desert, forest, canyon, or mountain hike.

GETTING THERE
The description of the road to the trailhead starts from the nearest town or major highway intersection. You'll also find the elevation of the trailhead here in feet and the GPS coordinates for the trailhead in latitude and longitude.

THE TRAIL
Here's the meat of the hike description, the detailed, turn-by-turn narrative. I include distances to each trail junction, which correspond to the mileage

ticks on the trail map included with each hike. I also describe the trail and turns in terms of landmarks where possible, so you can confirm your trail navigation. Remember that trail signs can be missing or incorrect.

GOING FARTHER

If the main hike is not enough and you're hungry for more, look in this section for side hikes, extensions, and other options to make the hike longer. Remember that these additions will not only make the hike longer but may also make it more difficult.

Be Careful

Reasonably fit, experienced, and well-equipped hikers rarely make headlines by calling for a rescue. It's usually the unprepared who get into trouble. Just because you can walk doesn't mean you can handle running out of water, losing the trail, or sudden changes in the weather.

Remember that all but the easiest trails can quickly take you into remote country where you are on your own. Even many Arizona trailheads are in remote places where a vehicle breakdown will require you to walk several miles to the nearest town or highway.

It's always best to hike with one or two other people. While solo hiking is very rewarding and I've done plenty of it, you *must* always leave a description of your route, the time you plan to return, and when and who to call if you are overdue. This "flight plan" for your hike is a good idea even if you're hiking with other people.

On all hikes that take you away from civilization, you should carry the following essentials. Backpackers will need a bit more gear, of course.

ESSENTIALS

🚶 Water. In Arizona, water is the most important item in your pack because of the hot summer weather, low humidity, and scarcity of trailside springs and creeks. The onset of dehydration and heat exhaustion is insidious and can lead to sunstroke, a life-threatening medical emergency that requires immediate transport to a hospital. To prevent dehydration, always carry and drink more water than you think you'll need. See the following Water section for more information.

🚶 Topographic map. Carry and know how to read a topo map. GPS maps, while very useful, are no substitute for printed maps because they don't show the big picture of surrounding terrain and landmarks, and because GPS receivers can fail.

🚶 Compass. As with maps, a GPS receiver with an electronic compass is a very useful tool, but you should always have a high-quality, liquid-filled, orienteering-style compass in your pack. I recommend a compass with a built-in declination offset. This means you can set the compass to read true north, the same as your map. The last thing you need when you're trying to sort out your position is to get confused converting magnetic bearings to true.

Also, note that lower-cost GPS units do not have magnetic compasses and can only show directions while you are moving.

I'm not slamming GPS. Many of the trails in this book were mapped with GPS and it is a remarkable tool, one that gives your position with stunning accuracy nearly anywhere on the planet. But like any other tool, you must learn its limitations as well as how to use it. In many desert areas, such as the Grand Canyon, navigation is primarily by landmarks and travel is limited by cliffs and canyons. Attempting to walk a direct GPS or compass course will fail, often in a dramatic fashion as you find yourself stopped by a 500-foot drop-off. In other places, such as slot canyons, the GPS receiver can't see enough satellites to get a fix. This is the case in hike #8 in this book, Paria Canyon. There, you must navigate by locating landmarks along the canyon and finding them on your topo map.

On the other hand, GPS can be very useful in forest or open desert plains and plateaus where there are few visible or nearby landmarks. The ability to confirm your location at the correct trail junction, and that you are progressing toward the next landmark or the end of the hike is extremely valuable information. Just don't let your traditional navigation skills get rusty.

𝕩 Extra clothing. Be ready for weather changes. On a warm desert hike where you're walking in shorts, this might include bringing a pair of long pants and a windbreaker, because the desert cools off very quickly at night. In the mountains, rain gear and an extra layer of insulation are always a good idea. Summer thunderstorms can drop a deluge in a few minutes and lower the temperature 40 degrees or more. In the spring, high winds often blow in the afternoon, resulting in serious windchill effects.

𝕩 Extra food. On day hikes, even if I plan to be back in civilization for lunch, I always carry a few energy bars, nuts, or other snacks just in case I'm delayed. On longer hikes or backpack trips, carry a little more food than you'll need, in case of delays or injuries.

𝕩 A flashlight—a no-brainer. It's just no fun and can be very dangerous to be caught out after dark with no light. The best lights for hiking are small LED headlamps that leave your hands free. Many of these run on several AAA-size batteries and have two or more intensity settings that let you save battery life for detail work or reading but still produce a bright light when you need it, like covering that last 0.5-mile of trail to your car in the dark.

🏃 A first aid kit. Various wilderness first aid kits are available, tailored for day hikers as well as backpackers. Have one in your pack at all times and also consider taking a first aid course periodically. Desert first aid kits should include good tweezers for removing cactus spines.

🏃 Matches or fire starter. Your ability to start a fire separates you from the wild animals. Unlike most of the local wildlife, you don't have much fur to keep you warm. In an emergency, a fire not only keeps you warm but also helps rescuers locate you. If you carry matches, they must be the wooden strike-anywhere type carried in a waterproof case. Disposable butane lighters are also excellent fire starters. Though they can run out of fuel or fail, this difficulty is overcome by carrying two or three of the mini lighters. The spark from a butane lighter will light a camp stove even if the lighter is out of fuel. Magnesium fire starters produce a hot, reliable spark even when wet, but starting a fire requires fine, dry tinder and some skill.

🏃 A folding pocketknife with at least one good, sharp blade does the trick for fixing broken shoelaces, shaving dry tinder to start a fire in an emergency, and cutting cheese. Scissors are useful for such things as cutting moleskin to treat blisters. Most of the other tools, such as USB thumb drives, on Swiss Army–style knives and multi-tools add a lot of weight and aren't that useful in the wilderness.

🏃 Sunhat. Keep the intense desert sun off your noggin by wearing either a flexible broad-brimmed hat, or a "desert rat" style baseball cap with side and back flaps to protect your ears and neck. Plain baseball caps are nearly worthless for keeping your head cool and preventing skin damage.

🏃 Sunglasses. Arizona sunlight is intense even in the winter. You do both short- and long-term damage to your eyes if you don't wear sunglasses with UV light protection. Cheap sunglasses actually increase eye damage by filtering visible light but not UV light. This causes your pupils to open, admitting even more UV light.

🏃 Sunscreen. Desert hikers should routinely use a good quality sunscreen with an SPF rating of 30 or better. This not only prevents sunburn but also helps retard skin damage and long-term problems such as skin cancer. The best sunscreens use physical UV blockers such as titanium dioxide, although these are harder to find.

🏃 Other items. It's helpful to carry toilet paper in a plastic bag and possibly a signal mirror and a whistle for emergency use. During the spring in the desert and early summer in the mountains, you may need to carry insect repellent for gnats and mosquitoes.

🏃 Backpacking gear. Backpackers have more fun with light packs. Figuring out what is essential while leaving behind the nice-to-have is a highly gratifying art practiced by most experienced backpackers. This skill is even more important in the desert where you often have to carry more water than hikers in wet climates.

Although there is a wide selection of lightweight and even ultra-lightweight backpacking gear, weight still adds up. It doesn't help much to carry 100 pounds of ultralight stuff.

The critical items that you should choose carefully are your pack, shelter or tent, sleeping bag, sleeping pad, and footwear. Don't scrimp on the price either. Cheap gear is almost guaranteed to wreck your trip and can threaten your life.

A well-designed internal-frame pack almost makes carrying a load fun. Almost. And a pack surely is more comfortable if it fits you well and is designed for your anatomy. Look for a lightweight design and avoid unnecessary straps and attachments that are really meant for technical mountaineering.

During some seasons in the desert and mountains of the Southwest, there are no bugs and you don't even need a tent—a simple tarp or bivy sack does the job. That said, most backpackers prefer a tent. It only takes one mosquito to ruin your night, and a tent is easier to set up than a tarp. For Arizona hiking, where nights can be on the warm side, consider a lightweight tent with lots of netting in the upper panels for ventilation. Such tents can still be stormworthy if they include a full-coverage fly.

The lightest, most compact sleeping bags are down-filled and really not that much more expensive than synthetic-filled bags when you consider that down has more than twice the life of synthetic fills. In the relatively dry Arizona climate, down bags don't lose their loft to moisture accumulation as they do in wetter locales.

Since sleeping bags don't insulate well underneath you, you need a sleeping pad. Desert hikers are split between the comfort of self-inflating foam-filled air mattresses, and the utter reliability of closed-cell foam pads. If you do use a self-inflating pad, check the ground carefully for cactus spines and thorns before laying down your groundsheet or setting up your tent. And carry a repair kit.

WEATHER

Arizona's climate varies from low-elevation deserts that are scorching hot in summer to timberline country with arctic climates, with cool temperatures and even snow in the summer, as well as everything in between.

Summer temperatures reach as high as 128 degrees F in the lowest deserts during June. At the same time, the mountains and high plateaus top out in the 90s and usually are no hotter than the 80s. Summer nights can be chilly, even in the desert, because the dry air and clear skies allow temperatures to plummet after sunset. Temperatures can drop below freezing in the mountains during summer nights.

WATER

People doing strenuous work, such as hiking, require *two gallons* of water per person per day in summer desert heat. Of course, you're smarter than that and are going to hike in the mountains where it's cool, or plan desert hikes for fall, spring, and winter. But even Arizona's lush mountain forests have many desert characteristics, such as extremely low humidity much of the year. This means your body loses moisture insensibly, without sweating.

Backpackers can't carry water for an entire multiday trip, so desert backpack trips must be planned around water sources. Never depend on a single stream, spring, natural water tank, or other water source and always have a backup plan to reach another water source if your planned source is dry or you can't find it. For emergency use as well as backpacking, you should know how to find and use wilderness water sources. These include seasonal or permanent streams, springs, and water holes such as rock tanks and rain pockets. A description of the techniques for finding desert water sources is beyond the scope of this book. For that, refer to my desert how-to book, *Desert Sense*, published by Mountaineers Books in 2005.

Unfortunately, you can't just dip a cupful of water out of a spring or creek without taking a small but significant risk of contracting a waterborne disease. While waterborne diseases in Arizona are not life-threatening, contracting one can ruin your hike or vacation and recovery can take some time. So you should purify all wilderness water sources before using them.

The most practical, lightweight purifying system for both emergency use by day hikers and routine use by backpackers is chemical treatment with iodine or chlorine tablets. Modern chlorine tablets are the most effective of the two and don't have the problems of losing potency in storage as the old halazone tablets did.

Pump filters produce pleasant-tasting water but are heavy, bulky, and slow. They tend to clog readily in desert water, which is often silty. Also, very few filters are classed as "purifiers," which means they don't remove all disease organisms.

Bringing water to a rolling boil kills all disease organisms at any altitude, but is time-consuming, requires that you build a fire or use up stove fuel, and leaves you with hot, flat-tasting water. You can cool the water as well as restore the dissolved air that gives water much of its pleasant taste by pouring it back and forth between two containers. For these reasons, boiling is mainly useful in an emergency.

WILDLIFE

The most dangerous animal in Arizona aside from the one passing you on a blind curve on the drive to the trailhead is not the rattlesnake, but the tiny desert bark scorpion. This one-inch-long, straw-colored beast is nocturnal and likes to spend its days clinging upside down to the underside of sticks, rocks, or pieces of bark. Its venom is neurotoxic and potentially life-threatening to small children, the elderly, and others with compromised immune systems. But even healthy adults are going to feel pretty bad and should receive medical care as soon as possible. Larger, brownish scorpions are found nearly everywhere in Arizona but their sting is not dangerous to most people—just painful.

The black widow spider, found everywhere in Arizona and recognized by the red hourglass-shaped mark on its underside, is also dangerous. They aren't much of a hazard in the wilderness, though—most bites happen around woodpiles, old sheds, and other places that provide lots of spider hiding places.

Brown recluse spiders produce a nasty wound that takes a long time to heal but are not otherwise dangerous.

Fortunately, stings from scorpions and other dangerous insects and spiders are preventable by the simple expedient of always looking where you place your hands and feet. When picking up rocks to weight down your tent or firewood, kick them first. During the summer in the desert, when most wildlife is nocturnal, sleep in a net tent rather than on the desert floor.

Rattlesnakes produce a lot of unreasonable fear but most bites are suffered by people attempting to tease or handle a snake. A little understanding of rattlesnake behavior goes a long way in preventing unpleasant encounters. First, rattlesnakes are cold-blooded and tend to be found in environments where they can keep their body temperatures around 80 degrees F. During cool weather, this means they'll be out sunning themselves on open ground or rock slabs. In hot weather they'll hang out in the shade under rocks, overhangs, and logs. Rattlesnakes usually hibernate during the winter. If lizards are active, you can assume that rattlesnakes are active also.

Rattlesnakes sense you by feeling ground vibrations with their bodies, and generally move away long before you are aware of them. If you get too close, rattlesnakes warn you with their unmistakable rattle. If you hear a rattlesnake, locate it visually before moving to avoid it. The location of the rattling sound can be misleading.

Rattlesnakes can only strike about one-half their body length, and since rattlesnakes longer than five feet are rare in Arizona, avoid placing a limb closer than about three or four feet to any potential hiding places.

Don't play around with any snake, even ones you think are nonpoisonous. All snakes will bite if they feel threatened.

If someone in your party does get bitten by a suspected rattlesnake, keep them calm and seek medical attention as soon as possible. Although many defensive bites are dry, with little or no venom injected, the venom is tissue-destructive and the deep fang punctures carry a serious risk of infection.

The largest predator in Arizona is the mountain lion or cougar. Heavily hunted until recently, they have mainly survived in the remotest canyons and mountains. You'll be lucky to see a track, let alone a live animal. Although there have been no recorded human attacks in Arizona, there have been in other states, so a few precautions are in order.

Mountain lions hunt deer from above by ambush, stealthily stalking their prey and positioning themselves to strike from above and behind without warning. Avoid places where you can be ambushed, such as rock ledges and banks or overhanging tree limbs above your route of travel, especially if you can't clearly see them. If you spot a lion or tracks that indicate it may be stalking you, stay in the open. Make yourself as large as possible by spreading your clothing, and keep children with you and dogs on a short leash. Never allow dogs to roam free in mountain lion country, which is generally rocky or brushy terrain with lots of cover. If actually attacked, fight back with anything at hand.

A more recent hazard is that of Africanized bees. Closely related to the domesticated European honeybee, they are indistinguishable outside of a lab, except by their behavior. Africanized bees are much more aggressive in defending their hive and will attack people or animals that come too near. Although I have yet to hear of an attack on a hiker in the backcountry in Arizona (most attacks have taken place in the desert cities, and are only fatal to those who are unable to escape), you should still take some precautions. Never approach any bees, swarms, or hives, including domesticated bees. Be aware of the sounds around you as you hike and move away from any sound of swarming bees. Again, keep your dog or pet on a short leash. If attacked, drop your pack, run, and protect your face and eyes. Do not swat at the bees—that only drives them to attack more furiously. Seek shelter in a vehicle or building if available—otherwise, head for thick brush or vegetation, which confuses bees. Africanized bees rarely chase more than 0.5 mile.

Poison ivy can be found during the warm half of the year along streams and dry stream courses at intermediate elevations (about 4,000 to 7,000 feet) in Arizona. Although not everyone reacts badly to the organic acid present on the stems and leaves, poison ivy is best avoided. The low-growing plant is easily recognized by its glossy leaves that grow in groups of three. Keep your dog on a leash and under control around poison ivy. Although most dogs are immune, they can transfer the acid to your skin. If you do touch poison ivy or think you may have, wash immediately with soap and water, or even plain water. Immediate removal of the acid can eliminate or greatly reduce the reaction.

To put all this in perspective, by far the most dangerous part of any hike or wilderness trip is the one I mentioned at the start of this section—the drive to the trailhead. Your odds of being hurt or killed on the road are many, many times greater than that of being attacked by a wild animal.

Blue lupine flowers splash mountain meadows with color during the summer.

GRAND CANYON

Running 277 river miles across northwest Arizona, the Grand Canyon is not a single canyon but rather a complex maze of side canyons, large and small. As a world-class destination, the Grand Canyon attracts four to five million visitors per year, so you might expect the hiking to be crowded. And it can be, on favored trails at popular times of the year.

As the wildest area of the state, the Grand Canyon region offers plenty of spectacular hiking. The catch is that there aren't as many trails as you would expect at a major national park, and most of the trails that do exist get little maintenance. Because of these factors and the vertical relief of the Grand Canyon, hiking within the canyon is demanding.

The trails suggested here range from easy walks along the North and South Rims to strenuous day hikes into the canyon and to multiday backpack trips. Trails on or near the North Rim are covered first, followed by South Rim Trails. Because of the great elevation range, this is a year-round hiking area, though winter days can be cold, even within the Grand Canyon itself.

GRAND CANYON

1. North Canyon Loop

RATING	🚶 🚶 🚶 🚶
DISTANCE	5.5-mile loop
HIKING TIME	4 hours
ELEVATION GAIN	2,000 feet
HIGH POINT	8,890 feet
EFFORT	Knee-Punishing
BEST SEASON	Summer, fall
WATER	Seasonal at North Spring
PERMITS/CONTACT	None/Kaibab National Forest, North Kaibab Ranger District, (928) 643-7395, www.fs.usda.gov/kaibab
MAPS	USGS Dog Point
NOTES	Leashed dogs welcome

THE HIKE

This scenic loop hike takes you down into North Canyon on the eastern edge of the Kaibab Plateau, through cool spruce fir and aspen forest, past a rare spring, and along the rim of North Canyon following a portion of the 817-mile Arizona Trail.

GETTING THERE

From Jacob Lake at the junction of U.S. 89A and AZ 67, drive south 26 miles on AZ 67 to a point about 1 mile south of Kaibab Lodge, then turn left on Forest Road 611. Drive 1.4 miles, then turn right and almost immediately left to remain on FR 611. Continue 2.5 miles to the trailhead. The access roads are dirt and may be impassable during winter or wet weather. Elevation 8,857 feet, GPS coordinates N36°24.919'; W112°05.368'

THE TRAIL

The Arizona Trail passes through this trailhead—the branch to the south will be our return route. Follow the North Canyon Trail down into North Canyon. The trail initially descends to the south, but then turns northeast and descends in a series of short switchbacks. At the **1.9-mile point**, the trail reaches the bed of North Canyon and turns upstream. The trail more or less follows the bed of this normally dry stream until near the head

Indian paintbrush grows in the rim forest and in the pinyon-juniper woodland below and is often one of the first flowers to bloom.

of the canyon. Here the trail starts to ascend the right-hand wall of the canyon, passing North Canyon Spring then continuing to the shallow valley at the head of the canyon at 3.9 miles. Turn right on the Arizona Trail, which heads generally north and skirts the rim of North Canyon. At 5.5-miles you'll return to your starting point at the trailhead.

GOING FARTHER
Using the Arizona Trail, you can go farther—a whole lot farther. Completed December 16, 2011, in time for the 100th anniversary of Arizona's statehood in 2012, the Arizona National Scenic Trail runs 817 miles across the state from the Utah border to the Mexican border, passing through Arizona's most spectacular scenery on the way. The dream of a schoolteacher from Flagstaff, Dale Shewalter, the Arizona Trail is now a National Scenic Trail and is maintained by a growing list of volunteers and organizations. The Arizona Trail Association coordinates activities involving the Arizona Trail.

If you're not up to the full 817 miles just at the moment, you can take a nice walk northward on the Arizona Trail through a couple of alpine meadows. Although you can continue to Utah, a good goal is the second meadow at the 1.9-mile point, which makes the round-trip hike an easy

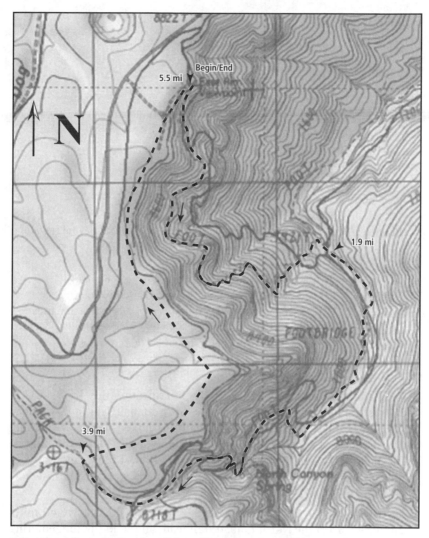

3.8 miles of nearly level walking. This pleasant walk is a great way to get a feel for the lofty alpine environment of the Kaibab Plateau, known as the "mountain lying down" to local Native Americans.

2. Ken Patrick Trail

RATING	🚶 🚶 🚶 🚶 🚶
DISTANCE	7.9 miles one-way with a shuttle
HIKING TIME	5 hours
ELEVATION GAIN	600 feet with many ups and downs
HIGH POINT	8,811 feet
EFFORT	Moderate Workout
BEST SEASON	Summer, fall
WATER	None
PERMITS/CONTACT	Entrance fee (Permit not required for day hikes)/Grand Canyon National Park, (928) 638-7888, www.nps.gov/grca
MAPS	USGS Bright Angel Point, Walhalla Plateau, Point Imperial. Trail is partially shown on topos.
NOTES	Dogs and pets prohibited on trails in Grand Canyon National Park. The North Rim is closed from mid-November to mid-May due to snow.

THE HIKE

Named after a park ranger killed in the line of duty, this trail starts at the same trailhead as the trans-canyon North Kaibab Trail and wanders across the Kaibab Plateau through beautiful mixed forest of quaking aspen, ponderosa pine, Douglas fir, and blue spruce before ending at Point Imperial, the highest point on the North Rim of the Grand Canyon.

GETTING THERE

From Jacob Lake at the junction of U.S. 89A and AZ 67, drive 40 miles south on AZ 67 to the North Kaibab trailhead, on the left before entering North Rim Village. Elevation 8,252 feet, GPS coordinates N36°13.045'; W112°03.370'

To reach Point Imperial, the endpoint of the hike, drive north 1 mile, then turn right on Cape Royal Road. After 5 miles, turn left on Point Imperial Road and continue to the end of the road. Elevation 8,800 feet, GPS coordinates N36°16.731'; W111°58.679'

Mount Hayden dominates the view from Point Imperial.

THE TRAIL

The trail heads generally northeast, staying on top of a broad ridge. After 1.4 miles, you'll pass the junction with the Uncle Jim Trail. Continue northeast on the Ken Patrick Trail as it skirts the head of Bright Angel Canyon while staying far enough from the rim that the canyon is not visible through the heavy forest. After the trail gradually turns to the east, it descends sharply and crosses the head of Bright Angel Canyon at 4.1 miles. After climbing out of the canyon, the trail heads east and crosses Cape Royal Road. At 5.0 miles, the Ken Patrick Trail reaches the North Rim of the Grand Canyon, then turns north to follow the rim. There are tantalizing views of the Grand Canyon along this section, but the heavy forest often obscures the view. Another factor is that the rim itself is not as well defined as the South Rim. This is because North Rim drainages such as Bright Angel Canyon flow into the Grand Canyon, breaking up the Grand Canyon's rim. In contrast, most South Rim drainages flow south away from the rim, leaving the South Rim itself generally more defined.

After 7.9 miles, the Ken Patrick Trail ends at Point Imperial, which is where you left your shuttle vehicle.

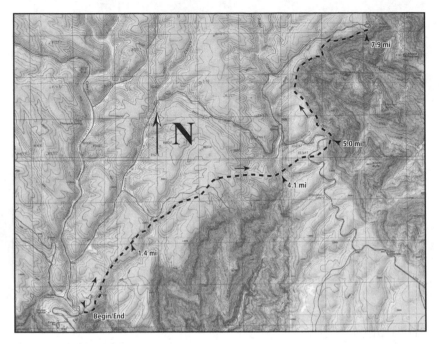

GOING FARTHER

There are four options for additional hiking along the Ken Patrick Trail. One is to take a hike on the Arizona Trail, which heads north from the North Kaibab trailhead and ends many miles north at the Utah border. Or you can take a shorter hike of up to 20 miles round-trip on the portion of the Arizona Trail within the park.

Another, much more strenuous option is to descend into the Grand Canyon on the North Kaibab Trail. Ultimately, this trail meets the South Kaibab Trail and crosses to the South Rim, a distance of 22 miles. But even a short walk into the canyon will give you a feel for its immense size. Just remember that the walk up is harder and takes longer than the walk down.

Another option is to leave the Ken Patrick Trail at 1.4 miles and hike the Uncle Jim Trail, a 5-mile side trip that takes you to the rim of Bright Angel Canyon.

Finally, a trail heads north from Point Imperial and connects to the head of the Nankoweap Trail at the park boundary. This is an easy 4-mile round-trip hike through rim forest that was partially burned in a recent forest fire. The Nankoweap Trail itself is a long, rough descent into the Grand Canyon and not a trail to be taken lightly.

3. Nankoweap/Saddle Mountain Trail

RATING	𝓧 𝓧 𝓧 𝓧
DISTANCE	12.2 miles round-trip
HIKING TIME	7 hours
ELEVATION GAIN	400 feet with many ups and downs
HIGH POINT	6,807 feet
EFFORT	Prepare to Perspire
BEST SEASON	Spring–fall
WATER	None
PERMITS/CONTACT	None/Kaibab National Forest, North Kaibab Ranger District, (928) 643-7395, www.fs.usda.gov/kaibab
MAPS	USGS Point Imperial
NOTES	Leashed dogs welcome

THE HIKE

This hike takes you to a remote viewpoint on the North Rim of the Grand Canyon overlooking the point at which Marble Canyon enters Grand Canyon.

GETTING THERE

Leave U.S. 89A about 20 miles east of Jacob Lake and drive south on Buffalo Ranch Road, Forest Road 445. Continue 27 miles to the Nankoweap trailhead. The access roads are dirt and may be impassable during winter or wet weather. Elevation 6,448 feet, GPS coordinates N36°20.825'; W111°57.152'

THE TRAIL

After leaving the trailhead, the Nankoweap Trail climbs gradually south as it passes through open pinyon pine and juniper woodland. When the trail reaches the west rim of Saddle Canyon, it descends to the normally dry streambed in a series of switchbacks. Turn left here, 1.0 miles from the trailhead, and follow the Saddle Mountain Trail southeast as it climbs out of Saddle Canyon. After passing through a saddle, the trail heads generally east as it climbs over ridges and descends into drainages on the north slopes of Saddle Mountain. As you continue, you'll have ever-changing views of Marble Platform and the distant Vermilion and Echo cliffs to the north and northeast. At the 4.5-mile point, the Saddle

Hiker approaching the rim of the Grand Canyon at the east end of the Saddle Mountain Trail.

Mountain Trail ends as it comes out onto the gently sloping plateau at the northeast base of Saddle Mountain. GPS coordinates: N36°19.757'; W111°54.413'. Note this point for the return and if you have a GPS receiver, save a waypoint.

Continue hiking cross-country to the southeast, staying right at the base of Saddle Mountain, until you reach the rim of a shallow canyon draining generally to the east. Cross this canyon and walk southeast out onto the point at the east end of Boundary Ridge. At **6.1** miles, this is your turnaround point.

You're looking down at the point where Marble Canyon ends and the Grand Canyon itself begins. The difference between the two is that Marble Canyon is a single main canyon with distinct tributary canyons, while the Grand Canyon is a complex of many side canyons, buttes, and mesas.

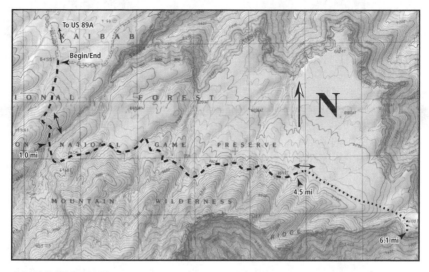

GOING FARTHER

The main Nankoweap Trail offers an interesting side hike. From the trail junction in the bottom of Saddle Canyon at the 1.0-mile point, turn south on the Nankoweap Trail and follow it up Saddle Canyon. The trail eventually leaves the drainage and climbs the ridge located just north, finally coming out into the saddle at the head of Saddle Canyon. This point on Boundary Ridge not only marks the boundary of Grand Canyon National Park but also the rim of the Grand Canyon itself. Turn around here to make this a 3.6-mile round-trip side hike.

Built by early geologists, the Nankoweap Trail is unmaintained and is one of the longest and roughest trails into the Grand Canyon. Only those prepared for a multiday backpack trip and having a permit from the national park should continue beyond this point.

4. Rim Trail

RATING	🚶 🚶 🚶 🚶 🚶
DISTANCE	Up to 7.4 miles one-way
HIKING TIME	Up to 4 hours
ELEVATION GAIN	300 feet
HIGH POINT	7,043 feet
EFFORT	Easy Walk to Moderate Workout
BEST SEASON	Year-round
WATER	Bright Angel Lodge near the start of the hike and Hermits Rest at the end
PERMITS/CONTACT	Entrance fee (Permit not required for day hikes)/Grand Canyon National Park, (928) 638-7888, www.nps.gov/grca
MAPS	USGS Grand Canyon. The trail is partially shown on the topo.
NOTES	Dogs and pets prohibited on trails in Grand Canyon National Park. Except during the winter, the free Hermit shuttle runs from the trailhead to the end of the trail at Hermits Rest, stopping at most of the viewpoints. You can hike as much or as little of the Rim Trail as you like, using the shuttle to hop between viewpoints and also to return to the trailhead at any time.

THE HIKE

This unique trail closely follows the South Rim from Pipe Creek Vista east of Grand Canyon Village to Hermits Rest at the end of Hermit Road west of the village. The hike follows the western portion of the Rim Trail from the Bright Angel trailhead to Hermits Rest. Although the trail is squeezed between Hermit Road and the rim, for most of the year private cars are not allowed on Hermit Road and public access is by free shuttle bus. This not only means you can use the shuttle bus to skip parts of the trail and return from the hike, but also makes walking the trail a much quieter and more peaceful experience. Oh yeah, and the views into the Grand Canyon are absolutely stunning.

The paved portion of the Rim Trail is open all winter.

GETTING THERE

From Williams on Interstate 40, drive AZ 64 to Grand Canyon Village. Or from Flagstaff on I-40, drive U.S. 180 and AZ 64 to Grand Canyon Village. Now comes the hard part. Except during the winter, parking near the rim or trailhead can be difficult. Continue on the main road through the village to Bright Angel Lodge and look for a parking spot there. If you succeed, walk west in front of the main lodge to the Bright Angel trailhead and the Hermit shuttle stop. Elevation 6,772 feet, GPS coordinates N36°03.458'; W112°08.641'

If there's no parking space in the Bright Angel Lodge lot, continue on the main park road to Maswick Lodge, which has a large parking lot where there are almost always spaces. Then ride the free Village shuttle, which runs all year, to the Hermit shuttle stop and transfer point.

THE TRAIL

The Rim Trail is paved where it passes by the Hermit shuttle stop but becomes a dirt trail when you follow it west. It also starts to climb, but don't worry, the hill in front of you is the only significant climb on the otherwise nearly level trail. The reason for the climb is that the portion

13

of the South Rim in front of you has been raised about 200 feet higher than the portion of the rim behind you by vertical rock movement along the Bright Angel Fault. This fault starts south of the South Rim and extends all the way across the canyon to the North Rim and beyond. Garden Canyon below you, as well as distant Bright Angel Canyon under the North Rim, have been carved along the weakness in the rocks caused by the fault.

Most of the named viewpoints are shuttle stops where you'll find a map of the shuttle route. The westbound Hermit shuttle stops at all stops, but on the eastbound return it stops at only Hermits Rest, Pima, Mohave, and Powell Points. If you decide to end your hike at one of the other shuttle stops, such as Trailview Overlook, you'll have to ride the shuttle west to one of the above points and catch the eastbound shuttle. Or just stay on the shuttle to the end of its route at Hermits Rest and ride it back to the Hermit shuttle stop where you started the hike.

Trailview Overlook spans east across Garden Canyon, the route followed by the Bright Angel Trail. This well-built mule trail is clearly visible below as it switchbacks downward, taking advantage of breaks in the cliffs caused by erosion along Bright Angel Fault. In fact, like most Grand Canyon trails, the Bright Angel Trail follows an old Native American route.

Continuing along the Rim Trail, at 1.1 miles, you'll reach Maricopa Point. Like many of the promontories along the South Rim, Maricopa Point is named for an Arizona Indian tribe. Maricopa Point looks almost directly down on The Battleship, a red rock butte formed in the Supai Formation on the west side of Garden Canyon.

As you head west on the Rim Trail, the path leaves the rim and skirts the old Lost Orphan Mine, a uranium mine that operated below the South Rim until the 1960s. Although the mine is closed and the property now part of the national park, the site is seriously contaminated with radioactive material and is off-limits to the public.

The Rim Trail returns to the rim at Powell Point, where a monument honors Major John Wesley Powell, who with his crew was the first person to explore, survey, photograph, and map the canyons of the Green and Colorado Rivers in 1869.

Follow the Rim Trail a short distance to the west to reach Hopi Point, which faces directly north and provides you with excellent views of the eastern quarter of the Grand Canyon, far to the west and to the east.

As the Rim Trail continues west, you'll find yourself looking off the edge of the Hopi Wall, the precipitous head of Salt Creek. At 2.8 miles you'll arrive at Mohave Point, another fine viewpoint, this time looking a

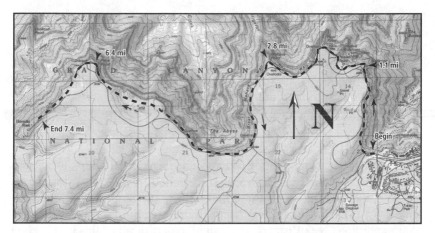

little more to the west than Hopi Point. If you're looking for a short hike, this is a good place to catch the shuttle, as the next major stop is 3.6 miles farther at Pima Point.

From here the Rim Trail follows the rim south along the top of the Great Mohave Wall. Ahead, you're looking into The Abyss, the steep head of Monument Creek. Along this portion of the South Rim, the cliffs below the rim are unusually steep and continuous. This is caused by the fact that several layers of shale, including the Toroweap Formation and the Hermit shale, are unusually thin in this area. Soft shale rocks erode readily and undermine the cliffs above. Where shale and other soft layers of rock are thick, they cause the cliffs above to recede so that broad terraces form, separating the cliffs. That is what gives the Grand Canyon its unique cliff-and-terrace appearance. But in The Abyss, the major cliff-forming layers such as the Kaibab limestone and Coconino sandstone nearly merge into a single cliff. Along this section The Abyss Overlook and Monument Vista are the only named viewpoints and shuttle stops, so you'll have several miles of quiet walking away from the crowds, even during the summer peak of the tourist season. Monument Vista is one of the few rim viewpoints where you can see a major rapid on the Colorado River. On a quiet day you can also hear the roar of Monument Rapid, almost a mile below you.

Pima Point falls at **6.4** miles and is one of the finest viewpoints along the South Rim. Looking down into the canyon to the southwest, you can see the remains of Hermit Camp, a tourist camp built along Hermit Creek on the Tonto Plateau about 1,500 feet above the Colorado River. An aerial tramway left the rim just west of Pima Point and spanned more than 4,000 feet to reach Hermit Camp. The tram was used to haul supplies back and forth. When the National Park Service completed the trans-canyon Kaibab Trail in 1928, it became the focus of tourism below the rim and Hermit Camp was abandoned a few years later.

One more mile of walking brings you to Hermits Rest at **7.4** miles and the end of the Rim Trail and the hike. This is also the trailhead for the now-abandoned Hermit Trail, which once served as the access to Hermit Camp and the Colorado River.

GOING FARTHER

An obvious extension of this hike is to return to the Hermit shuttle stop and follow the Rim Trail eastward. This section of the trail starts out as a paved, handicap-accessible trail and follows the South Rim for about 5 miles east to end at Pipe Creek Vista. There are shuttle stops at Yavapai Point and Pipe Creek Vista, so you can hike part or all of this portion and use the free shuttles to return. These shuttles run all year. The recently completed Trail of Time starts just east of El Tovar Hotel and runs to Yavapai Point. The Trail of Time interprets the geologic history of the Grand Canyon from its oldest rocks, created over 2 billion years ago, to the youngest rock at 270 million years.

5. Boucher-Hermit Loop

RATING   🚶 🚶 🚶 🚶 🚶
DISTANCE   18.8-mile loop
HIKING TIME   3 to 5 days
ELEVATION GAIN   3,700 feet with many ups and downs
HIGH POINT   8,890 feet
EFFORT   Knee-Punishing
BEST SEASON   Fall–spring
WATER   Boucher and Hermit Creeks
PERMITS/CONTACT   Entrance fee (Permit required for multiday hikes and camping in the Grand Canyon backcountry)/Grand Canyon National Park, (928) 638-7888, www.nps.gov/grca
MAPS   USGS Grand Canyon
NOTES   Dogs and pets prohibited on trails in Grand Canyon National Park. Except during the winter, the free Hermit shuttle runs to the trailhead at Hermits Rest.

THE HIKE

This rugged but extremely scenic hike uses three of the Grand Canyon's unmaintained trails to complete a loop through two major side canyons. There are also several side hikes, and you can easily devote five days to exploring this area. The Boucher is very steep in sections and much of the original trail construction is gone, so the loop uses this trail for the descent. The climb back out of the canyon is via the Hermit Trail, which was one of the last of the old trails to be abandoned and is in better shape.

GETTING THERE

From Williams on Interstate 40, drive AZ 64 to Grand Canyon Village. Or from Flagstaff on I-40, drive U.S. 180 and AZ 64 to Grand Canyon Village. Now comes the hard part. Except during the winter, parking near the rim or trailhead can be difficult. Continue on the main road through the village to Bright Angel Lodge and look for a parking spot there. If you succeed, walk west in front of the main lodge to the Bright Angel trailhead and the Hermit shuttle stop. Then take the Hermit shuttle to

Stormy skies over the Grand Canyon as seen from the Hermit Trail.

Hermits Rest and the Hermit trailhead. Elevation 6,637 feet, GPS coordinates N36°03.633'; W112°12.733'

Then ride the free Village shuttle, which runs all year, to the Hermit shuttle stop and transfer point.

During the winter the Hermit shuttle does not run. From Bright Angel Lodge, drive west on Hermit Road to its end and the Hermit trailhead.

THE TRAIL

Follow the Hermit Trail west down a couple of gentle switchbacks, then to the northwest. The trail works its way down through the upper cliffs of the Kaibab limestone and then descends to the west through the cross-bedded layers of Coconino sandstone. Serious trail construction was done in this section where the trail was paved with slabs of sandstone placed on end. Also watch for fossil footprints made by reptiles. The Coconino sandstone was deposited in a Sahara-like desert that once covered much of the Southwest, and the sloping layers in the sandstone are the faces of the ancient dunes. Fossil tracks always go down the face of the dunes, never up, because climbing animals destroy their own tracks.

Below the Coconino sandstone, the trail comes out onto red slopes eroded from the soft Hermit shale. Stay right at the junction with the

Waldron Trail at **1.0** mile and continue to the Dripping Spring Trail at **1.2** miles. This trail junction, on the rim of Hermit Canyon, marks the start of the loop hike. Turn left on the Dripping Spring Trail and follow it around the head of Hermit Canyon. In places the trail is on the edge of some impressive drops formed by sandstone cliffs in the Supai Formation below the trail.

At **2.2** miles, turn right on the Boucher Trail. The original trailhead for the Boucher Trail is left on Mesa Eremita but is seldom used today. Follow the Boucher Trail generally north as it skirts the west rim of Hermit Canyon. As you proceed you get good views of the Hermit Trail climbing up the opposite side of Hermit Canyon, and also of the layers of the Supai Formation. The Supai Formation consists of alternating layers of shale, sandstone, and limestone that were deposited in a fluctuating environment of shallow seas and tidal flats. When sediments were briefly exposed to the air, iron minerals oxidized and gave the future rocks their reddish color.

Trails and routes in the Grand Canyon are generally controlled by the location of breaks in the cliffs formed by the horizontal layers of sedimentary rock. Hard rocks, such as limestone and shale form cliffs from tens to hundreds of feet high, and soft rocks such shale and siltstone undermine the cliffs and cause them to recede, forming terraces. Terraces may be only a few feet wide or several miles. Terraces such as the one formed on the Hermit shale followed by the Boucher Trail are the usual route of travel through the Grand Canyon, whether on or off trail.

After the Boucher Trail crosses below Yuma Point, it heads into upper Travertine Canyon. At **5.0** miles, after staying on the same level for nearly 3.0 miles, it finds a break in the cliffs of the Supai Formation and starts an abrupt, steep descent. Most breaks in the cliffs of the canyon are caused by faults, where the rock on one side of the fault moved in relation to the other side. The movement weakens and shatters the rock, allowing erosion to form rockslides, ravines, and sometimes even gentle talus slopes.

At the base of the Supai Formation, the Boucher Trail follows the rim of the Redwall limestone northward. Actually a pearly gray in color on fresh exposures, the Redwall limestone is stained red by iron minerals leaching down from the Supai Formation. Deposited in a deep ocean and created from the shells of trillions of tiny sea creatures, the Redwall limestone is consistently 550 feet high throughout the Grand Canyon and forms a monolithic cliff. It is the most serious barrier to travel between rim and river.

The Boucher Trail heads over the saddle at Whites Butte at **6.5** miles. Pause here a bit and look behind you where the Boucher Trail descended the Supai Formation. The fault extends through the saddle you're standing on, then northward. This fault made the Boucher Trail possible by creating the break in the Supai Formation you just hiked as well as the break in the Redwall limestone you are about to descend.

From the saddle, follow the Boucher Trail north and down into a narrow ravine. As you descend in short, rough switchbacks, the walls of Redwall limestone begin to tower over you. At the bottom of the Redwall limestone, the canyon opens out and the trail descends the west-facing slopes toward Boucher Creek.

The slopes below the Redwall limestone are formed on the Muav limestone and Bright Angel shale. Muav limestone is greenish and mixed with shale. It forms stepped cliffs at the base of the Redwall limestone, along with narrow terraces. The Bright Angel shale is hundreds of feet thick in this portion of the Grand Canyon, and forms a broad terrace, the Tonto Plateau. The Tonto Plateau opens out before you as the Boucher Trail continues its steep descent.

The original trail was not as steep. Carefully constructed switchbacks moderated the descent angle, but modern hikers have cut these switchbacks and destroyed the old trail through erosion. They've also made the Boucher Trail more of a knee-grinder than it used to be.

At **7.4** miles the Boucher Trail finally levels out and meets the Tonto Trail. Follow the Boucher Trail left about 0.5 miles to Boucher Creek, a small permanent stream, and campsites on the terraces near the creek.

You can also explore remains of an old cabin and mine, about all that's left of efforts to exploit this area of the Grand Canyon. Louis Boucher, the "Hermit," constructed the Boucher Trail to reach mineral deposits in this area. He lived alone for many years and the nearby Hermit Trail was named after him.

To continue the loop hike, pick up enough water to last the entire day before leaving Boucher Creek. The next water source is at Hermit Creek. Now, retrace your steps up the Boucher Trail and then turn left onto the Tonto Trail. This trail takes advantage of the broad terrace formed in the Bright Angel shale to wander 72.0 miles through the eastern Grand Canyon, connecting many of the rim-to-river trails. Our loop follows a small portion of the Tonto Trail. Although used by prospectors and other early explorers, most of the Tonto Trail was never a constructed trail. Instead it generally follows the easiest route along the rim of the Tapeats sandstone cliff. The only visible trail construction is in places where the Tonto Trail crosses side canyons.

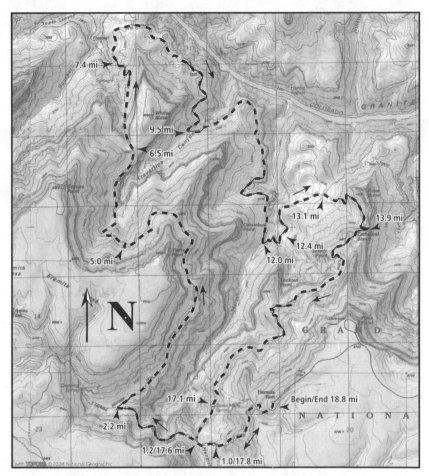

As you follow the Tonto Trail north and then east and southeast below Whites Butte, you'll soon realize two facts about the Tonto Trail and travel along the Tonto Plateau: The Tonto Plateau is not flat and the Tonto Trail is not straight. Tourists looking down on the Tonto Plateau from rim viewpoints thousands of feet above think it is flat. It is certainly much gentler than the massive cliffs above and below it, but it's all relative. Up close, the Tonto Plateau is actually hilly and cut by numerous ravines and canyons. As a result, the Tonto Trail never proceeds in a straight line. Instead, it constantly winds in and out of small gullies and large ravines, all the while working its way out to a point or back into the depths of a side canyon. There are places along the Tonto Trail where you hike 5.0 miles to travel 1.0 mile in a straight line. That is one of many reasons why hiking in the Grand Canyon is harder (and slower) than it seems. Patience is the key. Enjoy the ever-changing views as the trail wanders along the rim of Granite Gorge, 1,500 feet above the Colorado River.

As the trail skirts the rim of Granite Gorge, you'll get great views of the Colorado River. Granite Gorge itself is mostly carved from the gray-black Vishnu schist, a metamorphic rock that is the roots of an ancient mountain range. When the Vishnu schist was originally deposited 2.25 billion years ago as shale and siltstone, the only life on Earth was single-celled creatures in the oceans.

The brownish 200-foot cliff that forms the rim of Granite Gorge is Tapeats sandstone. The Tapeats sandstone was laid down at the margins of a sea that invaded the region and covered the Vishnu schist, which had been eroded down from a lofty mountain range to a sea-level plain. Look closely at the Tapeats sandstone and you'll see that it is composed of coarse sand grains that typically result when an ocean vigorously attacks a receding coastline.

Follow the Tonto Trail south into the recesses of Travertine Canyon, which it crosses at mile 9.5. This canyon is named for the large deposits of travertine, a carbonate rock precipitated out of water from springs and creeks. Though Travertine Canyon is dry today, the presence of travertine shows that water was once present in large quantities year-round. Springs and creeks elsewhere in the Grand Canyon are actively creating travertine deposits today,

After crossing the normally dry bed of Travertine Canyon, the Tonto Trail heads northeast around a point above Granite Gorge and then almost immediately heads south into Hermit Canyon. After a detour around a side canyon, the trail descends to the bed of Hermit Canyon at a point east of Columbus Point, at mile 12.0. Note the remains of elaborate trail construction dating from the late 1920s, when Hermit Creek was the site of a tourist camp.

Hermit Creek runs year-round and supports a desert oasis of cottonwood trees, birds, and other wildlife. Camping is allowed at only two sites, a campground along the creek just below the trail crossing, and at the Colorado River at the mouth of Hermit Canyon.

To continue the hike, follow the Tonto Trail east out of Hermit Canyon. On the slopes of the Tonto Plateau, you'll pass the remains of Hermit Camp at mile 12.4, a tent camp established by the Fred Harvey Company to accommodate tourists in reasonable comfort. The camp featured running water and a 4,000-foot aerial tramway, which brought supplies down from Pima Point on the South Rim. Hermit Camp and the Hermit

Trail were abandoned around 1930, after the completion of the trans-canyon Kaibab Trail moved the focus of below-the-rim tourism to that area.

Follow the Tonto Trail north and eastward to a saddle where you'll turn right onto the Hermit Trail at mile 13.1. As the last of the old can-yon trails to be abandoned, the Hermit Trail is in better shape than most of the canyon's unmaintained trails. Now very popular with backpack-ers, the trail climbs out of the canyon at a steadier grade than the steep Boucher Trail.

Broad switchbacks take you up the slopes of Bright Angel shale toward the imposing cliffs of Muav and Redwall limestone. The Hermit Trail ascends the Redwall limestone on tight switchbacks known as Cathedral Stairs at mile 13.9. At the top of the Redwall limestone the Hermit Trail heads generally southwest along the slopes of the Supai Formation, tak-ing advantage of breaks in the cliffs to climb up to higher terraces. (The trail doesn't manage to break through the last of the Supai Formation until after it passes the old shelter at Santa Maria Spring at mile 17.1.) The spring is now an unreliable seep, so don't depend on it for water.

After a final series of switchbacks through the upper Supai cliff, you'll close the loop at the junction with the Dripping Springs Trail in Hermit Basin at mile 17.5. Turn left to retrace your steps and ascend the upper Hermit Trail to the Hermit trailhead.

GOING FARTHER

There are several optional side hikes you can take. From the remains of Boucher's old mining camp, you can follow the Tonto Trail down Boucher Creek to the confluence with Topaz Canyon, then follow Boucher Creek to the Colorado River. This is an easy cross-country walk along the gravel streambed and the round-trip hike only takes a couple of hours.

From the campground at Hermit Camp, you can follow Hermit Creek to the Colorado River. Although a trail was built during the tourist camp days, floods have destroyed nearly all traces and the walk is essentially cross-country, though not difficult. As the gorge of lower Hermit Canyon deepens and you near the Colorado River, the first warning that the river is near is the increasing roar of Hermit Rapids, one of the largest rapids on the river within the Grand Canyon. At high water, the waves of Her-mit Rapids can reach 30 feet.

6. South Kaibab–Bright Angel Trails

RATING	🚶 🚶 🚶 🚶 🚶
DISTANCE	14.2 miles one-way
HIKING TIME	2 or 3 days
ELEVATION GAIN	4,290 feet
HIGH POINT	6,715 feet
EFFORT	Knee-Punishing
BEST SEASON	Fall–spring
WATER	Bright Angel Campground, Indian Garden Campground
PERMITS/CONTACT	Entrance fee (Permit required for multiday hikes and camping in the Grand Canyon backcountry)/Grand Canyon National Park, (928) 638-7888, www.nps.gov/grca
MAPS	USGS Grand Canyon, Phantom Ranch
NOTES	Dogs and pets prohibited on trails in Grand Canyon National Park. Park at Bright Angel trailhead or elsewhere in Grand Canyon Village and ride the free Village and Kaibab Trail shuttles to reach the starting point.

THE HIKE

This hike uses the park's only maintained trail system to take you to the bottom of the canyon and back. The descent along the South Kaibab Trail is especially scenic because the trail spends much of its time on ridges. The Bright Angel Trail is used for the climb out of the canyon because it features a gentler grade, and water and camping are available along the trail at Indian Garden. The South Kaibab Trail was built by the National Park Service as an alternative route to the Bright Angel Trail, which was privately owned when the park was created in 1919. Unlike most Grand Canyon trails that follow natural fault lines, the South and North Kaibab trails are engineered routes, blasted out of the cliffs.

GETTING THERE

From Williams on Interstate 40, drive AZ 64 to Grand Canyon Village. Or from Flagstaff on I-40, drive U.S. 180 and AZ 64 to Grand Canyon

Hikers descending the South Kaibab Trail.

Village. Now comes the hard part. Except during the winter, parking near the rim or Bright Angel trailhead can be difficult. Continue on the main road through the village to Bright Angel Lodge and look for a parking spot there. If you succeed, walk west in front of the main lodge to the Bright Angel trailhead and the Hermit shuttle stop. This will be the end of the hike. Elevation 6,772 feet, GPS coordinates N36°03.458'; W112°08.641'

To reach the Kaibab trailhead and the start of the hike, take the free Village shuttle to Canyon View Information Plaza, then board the Kaibab shuttle to reach the Kaibab trailhead. Elevation 7,204 feet, GPS coordinates N36°03.197'; W112°05.022'

If there's no parking space in the Bright Angel Lodge lot, continue on the main park road to Maswick Lodge, which has a large parking lot with plenty of spaces. Then take the free Village shuttle to Canyon View Information Plaza and board the free Kaibab shuttle to reach the Kaibab trailhead.

After the hike, board the Village shuttle at the Bright Angel trailhead and take it to the Maswick Lodge parking lot to retrieve your vehicle.

THE TRAIL

The South Kaibab Trail drops off the rim into a series of short switch-backs that descend through the cliffs of the Kaibab limestone. (For more information on the rock layers in the Grand Canyon, see the Boucher-Hermit Loop, hike #5 in this guide.) Then, the well-maintained trail heads north and descends along the slopes of the Toroweap Formation. The trail comes out onto the ridge north of Yaki Point and works its way down through the buff-colored Coconino sandstone. The views are stunning as the trail continues to descend through the red layers of the Supai Formation. After the trail comes out onto a place known as Cedar Ridge, it skirts massive O'Neill Butte on the east, continuing its steady descent.

In fact, the South Kaibab Trail has a very constant grade throughout its length. The only level section is along the top of the Redwall limestone north of O'Neill Butte. At the end of this flat section the South Kaibab Trail abruptly descends the 550-foot cliffs of the Redwall limestone via short switchbacks down an east-facing obscure break. As the trail turns north and continues the descent along the slopes of the Tonto Plateau, watch for a small natural arch on the skyline of the Redwall limestone cliff to the west.

The trail continues north toward the rim of Granite Gorge, crossing the Tonto Trail at 3.7 miles. At The Tipoff, the South Kaibab Trail starts its final descent, passing through colorful, tilted layers of the Grand Canyon Series. These rocks were deposited on top of the Vishnu schist and then uplifted and tilted into fault block mountain ranges, much like the long, narrow mountain ranges found in Nevada today. Then the ancient mountains eroded to a sea level plain, leaving only a few remnants to eventually appear in parts of the Grand Canyon.

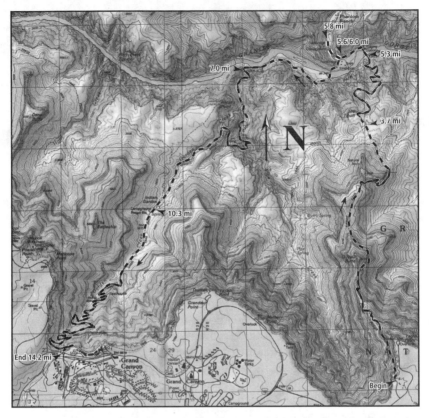

As the South Kaibab Trail descends into the 1,200-foot-deep Granite Gorge, you'll get impressive views both up- and downstream. You can also spot the two footbridges that span the Colorado River, the Black and Silver Bridges. Just above the river, at **5.3** miles, the trail goes through a short tunnel then crosses the Black Bridge to the north bank of the river to the start of the North Kaibab Trail at **5.6** miles. Follow the trail up Bright Angel Creek a short distance to Bright Angel Campground at **5.8** miles. There is also a ranger station, as well as Phantom Ranch, which has overnight cabins, a dining room, and a canteen where you can buy snacks and cold drinks.

Although many hikers spend the night at Bright Angel Campground, an alternative is to start the hike out of the canyon and camp at Indian Garden Campground on the Bright Angel Trail. This has the advantage of splitting the ascent over two days.

From Bright Angel Campground, hike south on the trail along the west side of Bright Angel Creek and turn right onto the River Trail at the corrals. Cross the Colorado River on the Silver Bridge, then turn right to stay on the River Trail. Another engineered trail, the River Trail was literally blasted out of the steep buttresses of Vishnu schist to create a route along an otherwise impassable section of the river gorge. The trail descends to the river at the mouth of Garden Creek, where there is a rest house at the 7.0-mile point marking the bottom of the Bright Angel Trail.

Warning: Do not wade or swim in the Colorado River. The river is extremely turbulent and hikers have drowned while attempting to cool off from the summer heat.

Unlike the Kaibab and River Trails, the Bright Angel Trail is a natural route first pioneered by Native Americans. The modern trail has been rerouted several times, and as you follow it up Garden Creek into Pipe Creek, you can see some abandoned trail work on the canyon walls high to the southwest. Switchbacks take you up the somber gray-black slopes of the Vishnu schist and then to the base of the Tapeats sandstone. Here you can literally put your hand across a gap in the rock record known as the Great Unconformity. This gap represents 300 million years of erosion where the ancient mountains were worn away before the horizontal layers of Tapeats sandstone were laid down in a sea.

Now, follow the Bright Angel Trail up Garden Creek to Indian Garden at 10.3 miles. This lush area is fed by a spring and was once farmed by Native Americans. Today there is a campground and a ranger station. The eastern branch of the Tonto Trail meets the Bright Angel Trail just before you reach Indian Garden, and the Plateau Point Trail heads west from near the campground.

Above Indian Garden, the creek is a dry wash and the last streamside vegetation disappears. The Bright Angel Trail continues up the slopes on the east side of the canyon and ascends the Redwall limestone on the slopes of a fault break. The Bright Angel Fault is one of the longest exposed faults in the Grand Canyon, extending across the Coconino Plateau well to the southwest of the South Rim and completely across the Grand Canyon to the northeast. Much of the Bright Angel Trail is built along the trace of the fault, where movement shattered the monolithic cliffs and created rockslides and slopes. Along upper Garden Creek, the rock layers to the west have been lifted more than 200 feet higher than the rocks to the east, which is very apparent where the trail climbs through the breaks.

As the Bright Angel Trail heads deeper into upper Garden Creek, it continues to switchback upward through fault breaks and across the broad slopes between the major cliffs. It passes two rest houses, which provide welcome shade during the hot summer months, and finally climbs to the South Rim just west of Bright Angel Lodge at 14.2 miles. If you parked at Maswick parking lot, take the Village shuttle to your vehicle.

GOING FARTHER

There are a number of optional side hikes, the most attractive probably being the hike up the North Kaibab Trail to Phantom Creek. From Bright Angel Campground, hike north 1.4 miles on the North Kaibab Trail. After passing the cabins of Phantom Ranch, you'll leave this last outpost of civilization behind. Gradually the towering cliffs of Vishnu schist become steeper, until the trail enters an impressive narrows known as The Box. Here, Phantom Canyon enters from the right. A short walk up Phantom Creek reveals the depths of this even narrower canyon.

Another, more strenuous side hike also starts up the North Kaibab Trail from Bright Angel Campground. After 0.7 mile, turn right on the Clear Creek Trail. Built by the Civilian Conservation Corps in the 1930s, this abandoned trail is still in good shape. The Clear Creek Trail ends at Clear Creek, 7.8 miles to the east, but a great hike follows the trail to an overlook at the base of the Tapeats sandstone, 1.6 miles from Bright Angel Campground and a climb of 1,060 feet. From this vantage point you have dramatic views of Granite Gorge both up- and downriver, as well as Bright Angel Canyon and The Box.

7. Horseshoe Mesa

RATING	𝕏 𝕏 𝕏 𝕏 𝕏
DISTANCE	4.8 miles round-trip
HIKING TIME	5 hours
ELEVATION GAIN	2,420 feet
HIGH POINT	7,390 feet
EFFORT	Knee-Punishing
BEST SEASON	Spring, fall
WATER	Miners and Cottonwood Spring, both well off the trail
PERMITS/CONTACT	Entrance fee (Permit required for multiday hikes and camping in the Grand Canyon backcountry)/Grand Canyon National Park, (928) 638-7888, www.nps.gov/grca
MAPS	USGS Grandview Point, Cape Royal
NOTES	Dogs and pets prohibited on trails in Grand Canyon National Park. Camping on Horseshoe Mesa is restricted to the designated campground.

THE HIKE

This strenuous day hike leads to the site of the Last Chance copper mine on Horseshoe Mesa. Now a protected historic site, the ruins of some of the mine works are still visible. The Grandview Trail, though officially abandoned, is in relatively good shape and easy to follow.

GETTING THERE

From Grand Canyon Village on the South Rim, drive south on the main park road and then turn east on Desert View Drive (also known as East Rim Drive). Drive 9.2 miles east and turn left on the road to Grandview Point. Park at the end of the road. Elevation 7,386 feet, GPS N35°59.887', W111°59.264'

THE TRAIL

The Grandview Trail starts from the right side of the barrier wall at the viewpoint and descends the slopes in the Kaibab limestone via a series of switchbacks. There are sections of serious trail construction where

A hiker on the Grandview Trail descends through the Kaibab limestone.

the trail is laid on cribs of logs lashed to the cliffs. Eventually the trail works its way down to an impressive notch at the base of the Coconino sandstone at the head of Cottonwood Creek. After this point the descent is straightforward as the Grandview Trail picks its way down the slopes of the red Hermit shale and Supai Formation. The trail descends onto the top of the Redwall limestone as it comes out onto aptly named Horseshoe Mesa. A fenced-off spot marks one of the shafts of the Last Chance Mine. Follow the trail north past the ruins of the cook shack to the campground, a good destination for the hike at 2.4 miles.

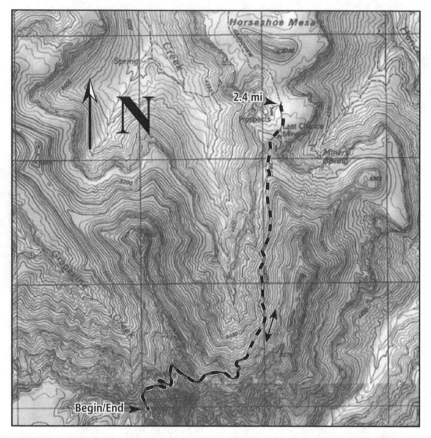

GOING FARTHER

Most day hikers spend their time exploring the ruins of the mine, but if you want to hike a little farther, take the East Grandview Trail off the east side of Horseshoe Mesa near the fenced-off mine shaft. This rough 1.25-mile trail passes by spur trails to the two main horizontal shafts of the mine at 0.3 miles. Stay out of all mine shafts—they are extremely dangerous. After the East Grandview Trail descends to the bottom of the side canyon, a spur trail at 0.5 miles climbs southeast to Miners Spring, which once supplied most of the water for the mining camp on Horseshoe Mesa. The trail ends on the Tonto Plateau at the Tonto Trail at 1.25 miles.

The 1.4-mile long West Grandview Trail descends west of the cook shack and down into Cottonwood Creek to Cottonwood Spring at 1.0 miles, a seasonal water source. It then follows Cottonwood Creek to end at the Tonto Trail.

A third branch of the Grandview Trail heads north from the cook shack and descends inside the west prong of Horseshoe Mesa, also ending at the Tonto Trail after 1.5 miles.

Quaking aspen live only about a hundred years.

NORTHEAST PLATEAUS

P art of the extensive Colorado Plateau, northeastern Arizona is dominated by the vast Navajo Indian Reservation, which covers one-sixth
of the state. The Hopi Tribe also calls northeast Arizona home, and
claim to be the direct descendants of the Anasazi, the "ancient ones"
who left the ruins of hundreds of cliff dwellings and pueblo-style towns
scattered across the Colorado Plateau when they abandoned the region in
the 13th century.

The plateau is a region underlain by generally horizontal layers of
sedimentary rock, including thick formations of sandstone. Flash floods
caused by late-summer thunderstorms, acting over thousands of years,
have carved hundreds of narrow slot canyons into the soft sandstone
of the plateau. Most hiking in northeast Arizona involves cross-country
hiking along canyon bottoms.

This section includes classic slot canyon hiking as well as easy walks
to some of the best examples of pueblo and cliff-dwelling structures in
the region. Slot canyon hikes must be done during warm, stable weather
in late spring or early fall, while the other walks can be done all year but
are best during warmer weather.

NORTHEAST PLATEAUS

8. Paria Canyon

RATING	🚶 🚶 🚶 🚶 🚶
DISTANCE	37.1 miles one-way with a shuttle
HIKING TIME	3 to 5 days
ELEVATION GAIN	1,180 feet
HIGH POINT	4,300 feet
EFFORT	Prepare to Perspire
BEST SEASON	April, May, October
WATER	The Paria River is brackish but can be drunk. Much better water can be obtained from unnamed springs, which are spaced about a day apart along the hike. All water must be purified.
PERMITS/CONTACT	Permit required for multiday camping trips/Bureau of Land Management, Kanab Field Office, (435) 644-4600, www.blm.gov/az/st/en/arolrsmain/paria.html
MAPS	USGS West Clark Bench, Bridger Point, Wrather Arch, Water Pockets, Ferry Swale, Lees Ferry; BLM Paria Wilderness
NOTES	Leashed dogs welcome. Because of the danger of flash floods in The Narrows from mile 5 to 9, you must have a stable forecast. Since the hike requires repeated crossings of the Paria River, wear river-running shoes, not conventional hiking boots. GPS receivers do not work in most of Paria Canyon due to the limited view of the sky.

THE HIKE

Paria Canyon is one of the longest slot canyon hikes in the world. At the same time, the hiking is relatively easy considering that it is mostly cross-country. In the narrowest part of the canyon, the sandstone walls are less than 20 feet apart and tower more than 500 feet above you.

GETTING THERE

This hike requires a car shuttle. If you have two vehicles, leave one at the Lees Ferry trailhead and drive to White House Ruin trailhead to start the hike. If you have just one vehicle, you can hire a shuttle service. For the current list, call the BLM at (435) 644-4600, or visit www.blm.gov/az/st /en/arolrsmain/paria/shuttles.html

To reach the Lees Ferry trailhead from Page, drive 24 miles south on U.S. 89. Turn right on U.S. 89A, drive 14.3 miles, then turn right on Lees Ferry Road. Continue 5.5 miles to the long-term parking area. Elevation 3,130 feet, GPS coordinates N36°51.948'; W111°35.534'

To reach the White House Ruin trailhead from Page, drive 29 miles west on U.S. 89 and turn left. Stop at the White House contact station to pick up your permit and check the weather forecast, then continue to the end of the road, which is 2 miles from the highway. Elevation 4,320 feet, GPS coordinates N37°04.760'; W111°53.408'

THE TRAIL

From White House Ruin trailhead, the hike starts as an easy walk down the broad bed of the Paria River. The width of the riverbed shows how large the river can become when it is flooding, but during good hiking conditions the Paria River is just a few inches deep and 10 or 20 feet wide. As you continue downstream to the south, the wash narrows and the canyon walls gradually become higher.

At about mile 5.0 the narrows begin as the vertical canyon walls close in. As you continue downstream, following the twists and turns, the canyon gradually becomes deeper and narrower until you reach the narrowest section at 7.2 miles. Here, Buckskin Canyon enters from the right through an even narrower slot canyon. In a pinch, there is a terrace with campsites that are safely above floodwaters about 0.2 mile up Buckskin Canyon, but normally these limited sites should be avoided as they are the only campsites for hikers coming down Buckskin Canyon to the confluence with the Paria River.

As you continue down Paria Canyon, the walls become wider but even higher and more spectacular. Around mile 8.8 the canyon becomes wide enough so that the first terraces appear, graced with cottonwood trees, willows, and other riparian vegetation. These provide the first good campsites that are safely above flood level, and you'll also encounter the first springs on the right canyon wall. Even if you don't camp right away, fill up with enough water to last through the next day.

The canyon walls are now over 500 feet high and continue to get higher as you hike downstream. At each bend on the river, the outside wall overhangs the river so that the sky is a narrow strip far overhead. The insides of the bends tend to have terraces with bright green cottonwoods standing in contrast to the salmon-colored Navajo sandstone that dominates Paria Canyon. At mile 19.3, watch for a narrow slot canyon

Hikers in Paria Canyon are dwarfed by the massive sandstone walls.

on the right. Informally called The Hole, there is usually a spring in the back of this short side canyon.

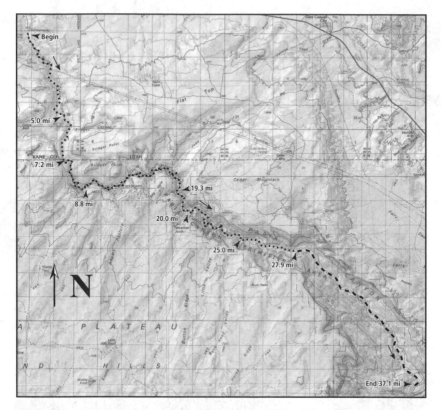

At mile **20.0**, just over the halfway point, Wrather Arch Canyon also enters from the right. An informal but clear trail leads up this side canyon less than a mile to Wrather Arch, a massive arch shaped like a stone jug handle.

As you continue downstream, the canyon walls now tower more than 1,300 feet above the bed. At approximately the **25.0**-mile point, you'll pass the last reliable spring on the left side of the canyon. From here to the end of the hike, the only reliable water source is the Paria River, so fill up here for your last night's camp.

At **27.9** miles, a side canyon comes in from the right and marks the point where an informal trail offers better hiking than the riverbed. In less than a mile the trail climbs above the riverbed and Paria Canyon turns southeast and opens up significantly. Soon you'll catch the first sight of the Echo Peaks about 8.0 miles downriver, which mark the end of the hike at Lees Ferry. The upper canyon walls continue to recede until they are several miles apart. This is caused by layers of shale and other soft rock that begin to be exposed at river level around mile 25.0. As more and more shale is exposed, the soft rock erodes easily and undermines the cliffs, causing them to recede.

The trail soon descends back to the riverbed and then alternates sides as it crosses the broad terraces on either side of the river. The remains of the historic Lonely Dell Ranch occupy the lower end of Paria Canyon and mark the end of the hike. Walk down the access road and turn left on the Lees Ferry Road to walk the short distance to the long-term parking lot and Lees Ferry trailhead.

GOING FARTHER

The main side hike along Paria Canyon is Buckskin Canyon. From the confluence, you can walk upstream where the canyon narrows to about 5 feet in width and 500 feet in depth. Although conditions change in Buckskin Canyon with each year's floods, usually the walking is very easy up the sand and gravel bed. The only barrier is a dry waterfall where hikers have cut steps in the rock. You can walk as far up the canyon as you want, but leave enough time to return to the confluence and hike downstream out of the narrows before camping.

The upper end of Buckskin Canyon is reached from the Wire Pass trailhead. Some hikers use Buckskin Canyon as an alternate start to the Paria Canyon hike. Because conditions vary, hikers must be prepared for canyoneering conditions, including swimming in cold, deep pools that sometimes form behind logjams.

9. White House Ruin Trail

RATING	🚶 🚶 🚶 🚶
DISTANCE	2.0 miles round-trip
HIKING TIME	2 hours
ELEVATION GAIN	400 feet
HIGH POINT	6,200 feet
EFFORT	Moderate Workout
BEST SEASON	Spring–fall
WATER	None
PERMITS/CONTACT	None/Canyon de Chelly National Monument, (928) 674-5500, www.nps.gov/cach
MAPS	USGS Del Muerto
NOTES	Dogs prohibited on trails in the national monument. This hike rates four instead of five because of the long drive to reach it, and the fact that it is the only trail open to the public in Canyon de Chelly.

THE HIKE

This is a short but very scenic walk to one of the most spectacular Anasazi ruins in the Southwest.

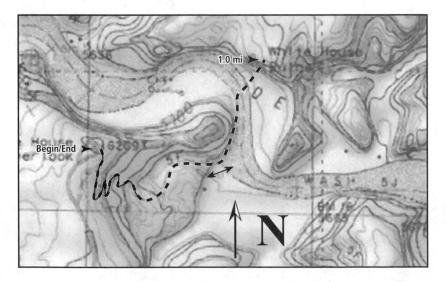

Multistory White House Ruin nestles under an overhang at the base of a 700-foot sandstone cliff.

GETTING THERE

From Chinle, drive 7.8 miles east on the South Rim Drive and turn left at White House Ruin trailhead and park. Elevation 6,195 feet, GPS coordinates N36°07.825'; W109°28.660'

THE TRAIL

Follow the White House Ruin Trail south and east from the parking area as it descends via several switchbacks. At the bottom of this descent the trail heads northeast down the slope and then crosses Chinle Wash at **0.6** miles. It then climbs a short distance to the ruins at the base of a 500-foot cliff, **1.0** mile from the trailhead.

10. Wupatki Ruin

RATING	🚶 🚶 🚶 🚶
DISTANCE	0.4-mile loop
HIKING TIME	1 hour
ELEVATION GAIN	Negligible
HIGH POINT	4,900 feet
EFFORT	Stroll in the Park
BEST SEASON	Year-round
WATER	Visitor center
PERMITS/CONTACT	None/Wupatki National Monument, (928) 526-1157, www.nps.gov/wupa
MAPS	USGS Wupatki SE
NOTES	Dogs prohibited on trails in the national monument

THE HIKE

This is a short, paved loop trail around one of the best-preserved ruins of more than 100 ruins in the national monument.

GETTING THERE

From Flagstaff, drive 12 miles north on U.S. 89 and turn right at the sign for Sunset Crater Volcano National Monument. Continue 21 miles

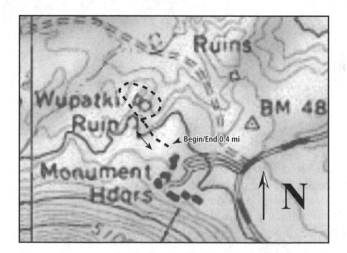

An easy, paved trail loops around the base of Wupatki Ruin.

to Wupatki National Monument Visitor Center and park. Elevation 4,907 feet, GPS coordinates N35°31.206'; W111°22.288'

THE TRAIL

Walk through the visitor center and out the rear doors onto the patio. The paved trail starts here and descends slightly to a point overlooking Wupatki Ruin. Take either branch of the loop trail to walk around the base of the multi-story ruin. A spur trail leads to a well-preserved ball court.

After the eruption of nearby Sunset Crater in AD 1066, the local Native Americans fled the area. After the volcano settled down, returning natives found that the volcano had deposited a thick layer of cinders and ash over the sandy soil in the area northeast of the volcano. This thin layer acted as mulch, holding moisture in the soil and making it easier to practice dryland farming. The result was a population boom that attracted members of all the major cultures in the area—the Hohokam from the south, Paiutes from the west, Anasazi from the north, and the local Sinagua. Artifacts found in the ruins at Wupatki show that the inhabitants traded as far south as the Mexico City area. Cultural influences from Mexico also show up at Wupatki, such as the ball court.

Quaking aspen has heart-shaped leaves that tremble in the slightest breeze.

SAN FRANCISCO PEAKS AREA

Located in north-central Arizona, the San Francisco Peaks (at 12,633 feet, the highest mountain in the state) dominate this region of volcanoes on the southern Colorado Plateau. There are more than 800 volcanic hills and mountains in the area, as well as canyons cut into the plateau.

The mountain's official name is San Francisco Mountain, but locals refer to the mountain as the San Francisco Peaks, or just "the Peaks." A network of trails covers the mountains and the adjoining Dry Lake Hills and Mount Elden, and this section includes a representative sample of these hikes. There are also trails on some of the smaller volcanic peaks, which are described here.

Southeast of the city of Flagstaff lies an area referred to as the "Lake Country" because of the unusual concentration of lakes found here.

While most of the Colorado Plateau lacks streams and lakes because of the porous bedrock, the Lake Country is covered by basalt lava flows from the volcanoes to the north, keeping more water near the surface. One of the hikes in this section follows the shoreline of Mormon Lake, the largest natural lake in the state.

Because of the high elevations, much of this area is snow-covered or muddy during the winter, so spring through fall are the primary hiking seasons.

SAN FRANCISCO PEAKS AREA

11. Bill Williams Mountain Trail

RATING	🚶 🚶 🚶 🚶
DISTANCE	7.0 miles round-trip
HIKING TIME	6 hours
ELEVATION GAIN	2,330 feet
HIGH POINT	9,256 feet
EFFORT	Prepare to Perspire
BEST SEASON	Summer, fall
WATER	None
PERMITS/CONTACT	None/Kaibab National Forest, (928) 635-8200, www.fs.usda.gov/kaibab
MAPS	USGS Williams South
NOTES	Leashed dogs welcome. Thunderstorms may occur any time but are most prevalent during summer afternoons from July through September. If thunderstorms are building, get off the summit and exposed ridges.

THE HIKE

This hike leads to the 9,256-foot summit of Bill Williams Mountain. Though adorned with radio towers and a Forest Service fire lookout tower, the summit offers panoramic views of the forested western Mogollon Rim.

GETTING THERE

From Williams, drive west on Bill Williams Avenue, then turn left at the sign for the Forest Service ranger station. Turn left at the next signed turnoff for the ranger station, then turn left again and drive to the Bill Williams trailhead. Elevation 6,921 feet, GPS coordinates N35°14.227'; W112°12.759'

THE TRAIL

Start on the Bill Williams Mountain Trail and follow it south across a meadow and into a pleasant mixed forest of ponderosa pine, alligator juniper, Gambel oak, and white fir. Several broad switchbacks lead to the junction with the Clover Spring Trail at **0.6** mile.

Aspens grace the north slopes of Bill Williams Mountain.

Continue to follow the Bill Williams Mountain Trail southward up the slope. As the trail reaches the steeper slopes of the mountain it drops into the canyon to the west. In the cool, north-facing recesses of this canyon, the forest becomes dominated by Douglas fir interspersed with the occasional stand of quaking aspen. A series of switchbacks finally lead up to the end of the trail at the Bill Williams Mountain Road, at **3.0** miles. Turn left on the road and walk 0.5 mile to the summit.

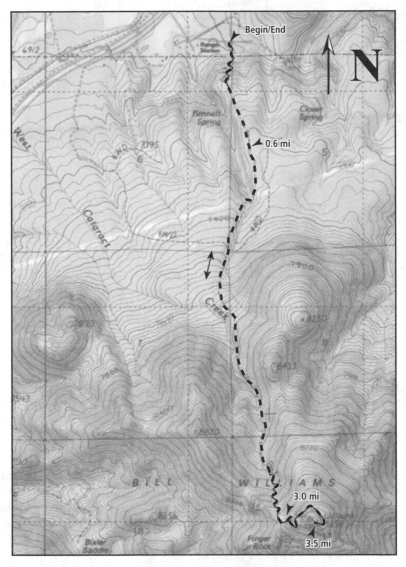

GOING FARTHER

An easy side trip leads 0.4 mile to Clover Spring, a small but significant water source on the Coconino Plateau. Because the surface rocks are porous, there is very little permanent surface water on the plateau. Clover Spring was an important water source for the natives as well as settlers, and is still vital for wildlife today.

12. Kendrick Peak Trail

RATING	🚶 🚶 🚶 🚶
DISTANCE	6.8 miles round-trip
HIKING TIME	6 hours
ELEVATION GAIN	2,710 feet
HIGH POINT	10,418 feet
EFFORT	Prepare to Perspire
BEST SEASON	Summer, fall
WATER	None
PERMITS/CONTACT	None/Kaibab National Forest, (928) 635-8200, www.fs.usda.gov/kaibab
MAPS	USGS Kendrick Peak
NOTES	Leashed dogs welcome. Much of Kendrick Mountain was burned in a lightning-caused wildfire in 2000. While much of the forest was destroyed on the north and east slopes, the fire stayed on the ground and left most of the trees intact on the south slopes traversed by this hike.

THE HIKE

This hike follows a good trail to the top of Kendrick Peak, Arizona's fourth-highest mountain at 10,418 feet.

GETTING THERE

From Flagstaff, drive 14.3 miles north on U.S. 180 and turn left on Forest Road 245. Drive 3.1 miles and turn right on FR 171. After 3.2 miles, turn right at the sign for Kendrick Peak Trail. Drive 0.5 mile to the trailhead. The access roads are dirt and may be impassable during winter or wet weather. Elevation 7,710 feet, GPS coordinates N35°23.215'; W111°52.078'

THE TRAIL

Follow the Kendrick Peak Trail to the east along the base of East Newman Hill through open ponderosa pine forest. Soon the trail meets an old, closed road and starts to ascend in broad switchbacks. After the trail reaches a saddle, it becomes a foot trail and starts to climb the south

Quaking aspen are the first trees to return after a major forest fire.

slopes below Kendrick Peak. As you climb, the forest becomes mixed, with Douglas fir and quaking aspen appearing. The trail switchbacks several times then heads northeast across the slope to a final switchback. Once past this last switchback, the trail turns northwest and you'll get glimpses of the summit, marked by a Forest Service fire lookout tower. The Kendrick Peak Trail emerges onto the east ridge of Kendrick Peak and a meadow at 3.1 miles. An old cabin here was originally the quarters of the fire lookout, but now he or she lives in the lookout tower.

The Bull Basin Trail branches right; stay left on the Kendrick Peak Trail and follow it west to the summit. Another trail, the Pumpkin Trail, starts at the summit and descends the west ridge of the mountain.

The fire lookout, not really a tower but a two-story structure with the glass lookout cab built on a cinder block base, is staffed during the summer fire season. Ask permission before climbing the stairs.

From the summit, you can see much of the Coconino Plateau. To the east, the 12,633-foot San Francisco Peaks dominate the view. South, you can see the southern edge of the Coconino Plateau and get a hint of Sycamore and Oak Creek Canyons incised into its edge. West, you can see two 9,000-foot mountains, Sitgreaves Mountain and Bill Williams Mountain. And to the north, you can see the cliffs of the North Rim of the Grand Canyon.

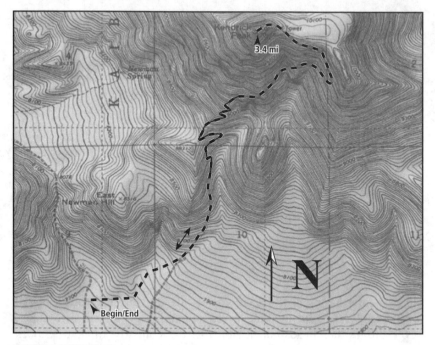

GOING FARTHER

As mentioned before, two other trails reach the summit—Bull Basin Trail and Pumpkin Trail. Both of these trails were heavily damaged by a wildfire in 2000. To get a view of a section of forest that was destroyed by the fire, hike north on the Bull Basin Trail along the north ridge of the mountain from near the old lookout cabin. Once a dense fir and spruce forest, most of the trees were killed by the intense crown fire. From the ridge, you can look down onto the northeast slopes, where new growth of quaking aspen is appearing, starting the regeneration of the forest.

13. Kendrick Park Watchable Wildlife Trail

RATING	🚶 🚶 🚶
DISTANCE	1.5-mile loop
HIKING TIME	1 hour
ELEVATION GAIN	Negligible
HIGH POINT	7,940 feet
EFFORT	Easy Walk
BEST SEASON	Summer, fall
WATER	None
PERMITS/CONTACT	None/Coconino National Forest, (928) 527-3600, www.fs.usda.gov/coconino
MAPS	USGS Kendrick Peak
NOTES	Leashed dogs are welcome but don't bring a pet if you expect to see wildlife

THE HIKE

This trail consists of two loops, a paved 0.25-mile wheelchair-accessible trail and a 1.5-mile dirt trail. Both trails skirt the edge of Kendrick Park and meander through beautiful mixed forests of ponderosa pine and quaking aspen. Small meadows and ragged outcrops of volcanic rocks add to the variety. Interpretive signs describe the natural and human history of the area. The best times for observing wildlife are early morning around sunrise and late evening before sunset. Walk quietly and carry binoculars for observing wildlife from a distance.

GETTING THERE

From Flagstaff, drive 19.8 miles north on U.S. 180 and turn left into the Kendrick Park Watchable Wildlife trailhead. The trailhead parking area is paved and has a pit toilet. Elevation 7,897 feet, GPS coordinates N35°24.134'; W111°45.411'

THE TRAIL

At the trailhead, an interpretive sign explains the trail and what to expect. Follow the paved trail to the right to start the loop. After about 0.1 mile, turn right on the dirt trail to walk the longer loop. When the dirt trail rejoins the paved loop, stay right to return to the trailhead.

Bright purple larkspur can be found in the summer in meadows at the margins of the ponderosa pine forest.

This area is typical of an "edge," where alpine meadow meets alpine forest. Edges are important wildlife habitat and support more diversity than pure forest or open meadow. Here you'll find great views of Kendrick Park and a few of the volcanic cinder cones in the area.

Some animals are commonly observed, while others are rare or retiring. Two of the most common are mule deer, marked by their unusually large, alert ears, and Rocky Mountain elk. The native Merriam's elk was hunted to extinction by 1900, so elk were imported from the Yellowstone area in the 1950s. Now the elk are so numerous that they are eating most of the young quaking aspen shoots and keeping these deciduous trees from reproducing. Along the outer trail, you can see an area the Forest Service has fenced to allow aspen to regenerate.

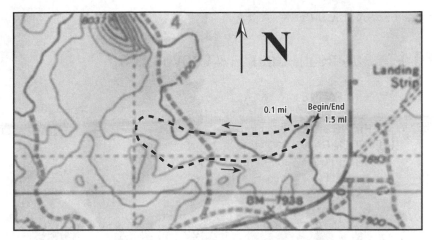

Another common animal you'll see is the Abert's squirrel. Easily identified by the tassels on its ears, this large squirrel is dependent on the ponderosa pine forest. You'll see the squirrels flirting their large, fluffy tails as they run across the forest floor and up the nearest tree, where they sit on a high branch scolding you. They have also been known to drop green pinecones on passing hikers.

Steller's jays are large blue jays with a crest on their heads. They flit from tree to tree and also like to scold hikers. The red-tailed hawk, one of the most common predatory birds, may be spotted soaring above Kendrick Park or sitting on a fence post. Marked by a reddish tail, these hawks sail the wind currents above open country, looking for lunch in the form of a rodent that lingers a bit too long in the open.

Another denizen that you may see out in Kendrick Park is pronghorn antelope. These fleet animals prefer to graze in large open meadows so they can spot predators from a long distance and then swiftly run to a safe place.

Novice hikers often worry about wild animals. Rest assured, the most dangerous part of any hike is the drive to the trailhead. As described in the Be Careful section at the beginning of the book, use common sense and recognize that wild animals are exactly that—wild, not tame. Treat all wild animals with respect and keep your distance, and you should not have any problems.

GOING FARTHER

Although there are no connecting trails, it is easy to explore along the west edge of Kendrick Park by walking north from the trail.

14. Aubineau–Bear Jaw Canyon Loop

RATING	🚶 🚶 🚶 🚶
DISTANCE	8.4-mile loop
HIKING TIME	7 hours
ELEVATION GAIN	1,800 feet
HIGH POINT	10,310 feet
EFFORT	Prepare to Perspire
BEST SEASON	Summer, fall
WATER	None
PERMITS/CONTACT	None/Coconino National Forest, (928) 527-3600, www.fs.usda.gov/coconino
MAPS	USGS White Horse Hills, Humphreys Peak
NOTES	Leashed dogs welcome. There is no access to Humphreys Peak from this trail. Cross-country hiking is prohibited on the San Francisco Peaks above 11,400 feet (timberline) in order to protect the San Francisco Peaks groundsel, an endangered plant.

THE HIKE

A great loop hike on the north slopes of Arizona's highest mountain, this is also a good escape from the heat during the hottest days of summer. Combine that with good views, historic tree carvings, and a beautiful alpine forest and you have a fine trek. This is also one of the best hikes for seeing fall color during October, when large stands of quaking aspen turn yellow, gold, and red.

GETTING THERE

From Flagstaff, drive north 19.4 miles on US 180 and turn right on Hart Prairie Road, Forest Road 151. Continue 0.7 mile, turn left on FR 418, drive 2.9 miles, and turn right on the Aubineau trailhead road. Drive 0.6 mile to the end of the road and the Aubineau trailhead. The access roads are dirt and may be impassable during winter or wet weather. Elevation 8,550 feet, GPS coordinates N35°23.130'; W111°40.619'

Hiking in Aubineau Canyon below Humphreys Peak.

THE TRAIL

From the trailhead, follow the Aubineau Trail east through the open ponderosa pine forest and down into Aubineau Canyon. The trail now turns
south and heads up the shallow canyon, meeting the Bear Jaw Trail at
0.5 mile. The Bear Jaw Trail will be the return trail; for now, stay right
and continue up Aubineau Canyon on the Aubineau Trail.

As you continue, the trail climbs steadily, the canyon becomes deeper,
and the nearly pure stand of ponderosa pines is gradually replaced by

59

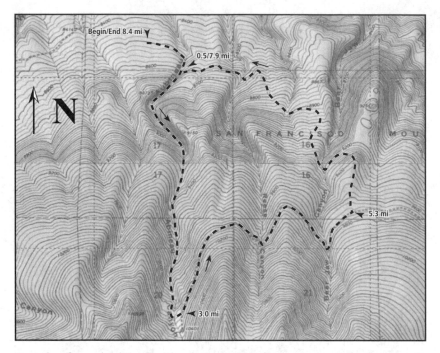

Douglas fir and white fir. The surest sign of your increasing elevation is the change in the forest. Quaking aspen soon appear, followed by Arizona corkbark fir and blue spruce. Limber pines also start to appear. At about 10,000 feet, the forest suddenly opens out at the lower end of an avalanche path. The trail skirts the west side of the avalanche path, then crosses it to end on the old Aubineau Canyon Road at **3.0** miles.

The old road was built as part of a City of Flagstaff watershed project in hopes of tapping into a spring in upper Aubineau Canyon. Unfortunately, these attempts destroyed the spring, but only after a pipeline was built around the north side of the mountain.

The view from this point is stunning. Humphreys Peak, the tallest peak in the state, towers over the head of the canyon. Several major avalanche paths start on the slopes below the summit and converge on the spot where you are standing. Evidence of these frequent avalanches surrounds you in the form of uprooted and toppled trees, flag trees with the branches stripped off the uphill side, and even large trees snapped in two.

There are dozens of major avalanche paths on the San Francisco Peaks, mainly on the north-facing slopes. Avalanches occur in all but the driest winters, and as you can see, many are large and destructive. In fact, avalanche conditions on "the Peaks," as they are known locally, are comparable with conditions in the southern Rocky Mountains of Colorado. The major difference is that no public roads or towns are threatened by these Arizona avalanches.

To continue the hike, turn left on the Aubineau Road and follow it north out of Aubineau Canyon. You'll see pieces of the abandoned water pipeline sticking out of the road in places, and there are access covers where the road crosses Reese and Bear Jaw Canyons.

At 5.3 miles, turn left on the Bear Jaw Trail, leaving the old road. The trail drops directly north down gentle slopes at first, but as the grade steepens, the trail swings west and crosses Bear Jaw Canyon. Watch for names and artwork carved into the soft white bark of the aspens all along the upper part of the trail. These historic carvings were made by Basque sheepherders who once grazed sheep on the upper slopes of the mountain during the summer. Don't be tempted to add your own carvings.

After the Bear Jaw Trail crosses Reese Canyon, it contours west to end at the Aubineau Trail in Aubineau Canyon, closing the loop at 7.9 miles. Turn right and hike 0.5 mile back to the Aubineau trailhead.

15. Humphreys Peak Trail

RATING	🚶 🚶 🚶 🚶
DISTANCE	8.4 miles round-trip
HIKING TIME	6 hours
ELEVATION GAIN	3,365 feet
HIGH POINT	12,633 feet
EFFORT	Prepare to Perspire
BEST SEASON	Late summer–fall
WATER	None
PERMITS/CONTACT	None/Coconino National Forest, (928) 527-3600, www.fs.usda.gov/coconino
MAPS	USGS Humphreys Peak
NOTES	Leashed dogs welcome. This hike rates four instead of five only because of the crowds using it as a workout trail. If you go on weekdays or off-season it easily rates five. Cross-country hiking is prohibited on the San Francisco Peaks above 11,400 feet (timberline) in order to protect the San Francisco Peaks groundsel, an endangered plant.

THE HIKE

This trail leads to the top of the highest peak in the state, 12,633-foot Humphreys Peak. The high point of the San Francisco Peaks, the summit gives you a 360-degree view of much of northern Arizona.

GETTING THERE

From Flagstaff, drive 7.2 miles north on U.S. 180, turn right on Arizona Snowbowl Road, and continue 7 miles to the first parking lot on the left at the ski area. The trailhead is located at the north end of the parking lot. Elevation 9,267 feet, GPS coordinates N35°19.867'; W111°42.700'

THE TRAIL

Walk a few steps to start the trail, which then heads northeast across Hart Prairie and enters the forest on the far side of the meadow. A series of broad switchbacks lead east up a broad ridge. As you climb, the forest changes from the mix of Douglas fir and quaking aspen at the trailhead

Humphreys Peak is the highest mountain in Arizona and has an appropriately commanding view.

to subalpine fir, Arizona corkbark fir, and limber pine. Limber pine is well named. The branches of this alpine tree are flexible, allowing the tree to shed the heavy snow that falls at this elevation and avoid being damaged.

As the trail nears timberline, the forest becomes dominated by Engelmann spruce and bristlecone pine. Bristlecone pines are among the oldest living trees. Although the bristlecone pines found on the San Francisco Peaks only reach about 1,200 years, their counterparts growing near timberline in Nevada and eastern California reach 4,900 years in age.

After the Humphreys Peak Trail swings into the head of the canyon above the ski area, a few short switchbacks lead to Humphreys Saddle, between Agassiz and Humphreys Peaks. This point, at mile 3.2, is also the junction with the Weatherford Trail.

Stay left and follow the Humphreys Peak Trail north up the rocky slopes above timberline. The trail stays on or near the main ridge, occasionally offering views into the Interior Valley. After the trail crosses several false summits, it finally ends at the highest point.

Like all the hills and mountains around them, the San Francisco Peaks are a volcano. The Peaks last erupted about 600,000 years ago in a huge explosion that took off the top 4,000 feet of the mountain, much like the eruption that collapsed the summit of Mount St. Helens in 1980. Later, glaciers carved out the Interior Valley, the northeast-facing canyon to the east. The Interior Valley is the southernmost glacial terrain in North

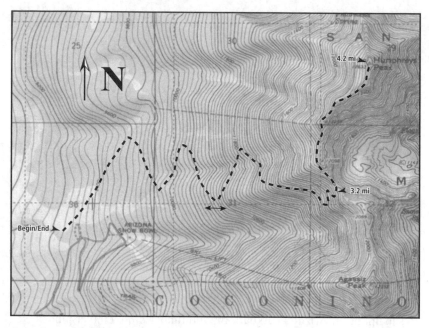

America, although there are no glaciers at present because the winter's snowpack usually melts away by August.

GOING FARTHER

The Weatherford Trail makes an interesting side hike. Originally built in the 1920s as a scenic road, the trail leads across the east face of Agassiz Peak, around the north slopes of Fremont Peak, then south to a trailhead at Schultz Pass. A 0.9-mile walk out onto the east face of Agassiz Peak takes about an hour and gives you fine views of the Interior Valley.

16. Kachina Trail

RATING	🚶 🚶 🚶 🚶 🚶
DISTANCE	9.8 miles round-trip
HIKING TIME	6 hours
ELEVATION GAIN	590 feet
HIGH POINT	9,225 feet
EFFORT	Prepare to Perspire
BEST SEASON	Summer, fall
WATER	None
PERMITS/CONTACT	None/Coconino National Forest, (928) 527-3600, www.fs.usda.gov/coconino
MAPS	USGS Humphreys Peak
NOTES	Leashed dogs welcome. Cross-country hiking is prohibited on the San Francisco Peaks above 11,400 feet (timberline) in order to protect the San Francisco Peaks groundsel, an endangered plant.

THE HIKE
This beautiful hike leads through the mixed pine, fir, and aspen forest on the south slopes of the San Francisco Peaks. Alpine meadows feature views of the forested Coconino Plateau to the south. Although the hike descends gradually to the turnaround point, the climb back is gentle and the trailhead at the ski area is accessible via paved road, unlike the eastern trailhead, which requires a high-clearance vehicle. This is a good hike for fall color.

GETTING THERE
From Flagstaff, drive 7.2 miles north on U.S. 180, turn right on Arizona Snowbowl Road, and continue 7 miles to the first large parking lots on the right at the ski area. The trailhead is located at the south end of the parking area. Elevation 9,399 feet, GPS coordinates N35°19.529'; W111°42.637'

THE TRAIL
Follow the Kachina Trail generally southeast through the forest. After crossing under a power line, the trail enters the Kachina Peaks Wilderness.

Fremont Peak as seen from the east end of the Kachina Trail.

At **2.4** miles the Kachina Trail crosses Freidlein Prairie, the first of several alpine meadows. These meadows are bordered with fine groves of quaking aspen, which break up the deep green of the surrounding evergreen forest with their gently trembling pale green, heart-shaped leaves. The leaves of quaking aspen are attached to the branches with thin, flexible stems, which lets the leaves move in the slightest breeze. In the West, aspens grow from the roots of other aspens, so that an entire grove is cloned from one

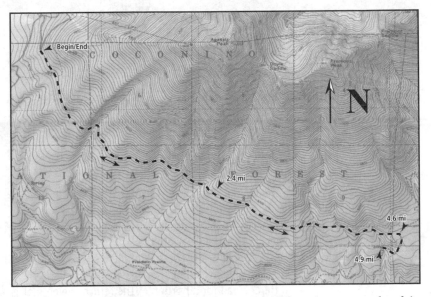

tree. That explains why, when the trees turn yellow, orange, and red in the fall, entire groves are a single uniform shade.

At **4.6** miles, the Kachina Trail meets the Weatherford Trail. You can turn around here, or hike to the actual end of the trail at **4.9** miles. In either case, return the way you came.

17. Inner Basin Trail

RATING	🚶 🚶 🚶 🚶 🚶
DISTANCE	6.5 miles round-trip
HIKING TIME	5 hours
ELEVATION GAIN	1,970 feet
HIGH POINT	10,530 feet
EFFORT	Prepare to Perspire
BEST SEASON	Summer, fall
WATER	Watershed cabins during the summer only
PERMITS/CONTACT	None/Coconino National Forest, (928) 527-3600, www.fs.usda.gov/coconino
MAPS	USGS Sunset Crater West, Humphreys Peak
NOTES	Leashed dogs welcome. The hike follows a slightly different trail for a portion of the return, which makes the return 0.1 mile farther than the outbound hike. Cross-country hiking is prohibited on the San Francisco Peaks above 11,400 feet (timberline) in order to protect the San Francisco Peaks groundsel, an endangered plant.

THE HIKE

This hike follows old roads that were built as part of the City of Flag-staff watershed project in the Interior Valley. Although not wilderness, the roads are closed to the public and the only vehicles you'll meet are occasional official vehicles checking up on the springs and wells in the watershed. This is another great hike for fall color.

GETTING THERE

From Flagstaff, drive 15.8 miles north on U.S. 89, turn left on Schultz Pass Road (a graded dirt road), drive 0.1 mile, and turn left on Lockett Meadow Road. Continue 2.1 miles, then bear left to remain on Lockett Meadow Road. After 0.7 mile, turn right to remain on Lockett Meadow Road. Follow the road to Lockett Meadow and the one-way loop road around Lockett Meadow and through the Forest Service campground. The trail-head is signed and is just past the first group of campsites. The access

Fremont and Doyle Peaks tower above Lockett Meadow at the start of the Inner Basin Trail.

roads are dirt and may be impassable during winter or wet weather. Elevation 8,560 feet, GPS coordinates N35°21.458'; W111°37.282'

THE TRAIL

Follow the Inner Basin Trail, an old road, as it climbs gradually up the broad floor of the valley above Lockett Meadow. As the trail meanders back and forth through the pleasant mixed forest of ponderosa pine, limber pine, Douglas fir, and quaking aspen, notice how the canyon floor is broad and relatively flat. When the trail skirts the sides of the canyon, the slopes above rise steeply and abruptly from the side of the canyon. This type of U-shaped valley is characteristic of glacially carved canyons. In contrast, valleys carved by rivers are V-shaped. Look closely at the soil where it is exposed in small gullies. You'll notice that it is composed of a random mix of large rocks, sand, and pebbles of all different sizes mixed together. This is another telltale sign of glaciers. As glacial ice moves down the slopes of a mountain, the ice scours the bedrock. Erosion on the slopes above the glacier brings down rocks of all sizes. This mixed load is carried downhill by the glacier. As a glacial period ends and a glacier melts away, it drops its mixed load onto the floor of the now-exposed glacial canyon. The resulting debris is called "till." In contrast, rivers and creeks sort their load of sand, gravel, and rocks depending on the velocity of the stream.

At **1.6** miles, the canyon narrows and you'll arrive at the watershed cabins. Part of the City of Flagstaff watershed project, these cabins mark

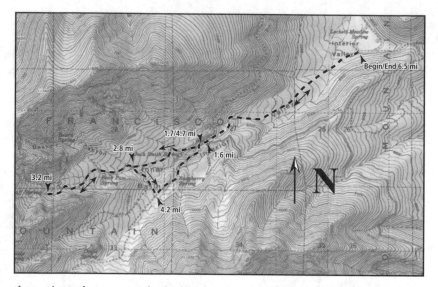

the point where several pipelines converge from the wells and springs above. The water is then piped along the Waterline Road to the left. When the pipeline is shut down for some reason, the water is often turned loose to flow down the ravine below the Inner Basin Trail. It soaks into the porous volcanic soil and vanishes after a hundred yards or so.

The largest cabin is a shelter for snow surveyors. Until the job was taken over by satellites, surveyors snowshoed and skied into remote mountain areas such as this to measure the snowpack. This data was used to predict the summer runoff. Since the majority of cities, towns, and farms in the West depend on the runoff from mountain snowpack for much of their water supply, this data is vital. Notice the small hatch above the front door of the cabin. This allows access to the cabin when the main door is buried. I've skied over the cabin when only 1 foot of the roof was exposed. A water spigot next to the cabin is the only accessible water source along this hike. All of the springs shown on the topo maps are capped and diverted and you can't get water from them.

The old Aubineau Canyon Road branches right, but continue straight ahead, up the valley, on the Inner Basin Trail. At **1.7** miles there is another junction; stay right on the trail to Flagstaff Spring. The old road on the left will be the return loop.

Follow the old road as it winds along the north side of the Interior Valley. Note the old, capped wells. Quite a few exploratory wells were drilled during the expansion of the watershed project in the 1950s, but only a few proved productive enough to pump. The first watershed project, in the 1930s, tapped the many springs in the Interior Valley. At the time, it was thought that the springs would provide an inexhaustible water supply for Flagstaff, but the city soon outstripped the capacity of the springs. After the wells were drilled, it was again thought to be enough water. Wrong! Now only about 1 percent of the city's water comes from the Interior Valley. The majority comes from reservoirs and several 2,000-foot-deep well fields on the plateau surrounding the city.

At 2.8 miles turn right at another junction in the old road system (the road to the left will be the return). Follow this road up the north branch of the Interior Valley to its end near Flagstaff Spring, the highest elevation spring tapped by the watershed project. A concrete box covered with a locked steel cover diverts the flow into a pipeline—you can hear but not see the water.

On the southeast slopes of Humphreys Peak, a major avalanche occurred during the record snow year of 1972–73. A climax avalanche roared down the slopes, stripping the snow cover to the ground and smashing into the old-growth forest just north of Flagstaff Spring. Trees as large as 2 to 3 feet in diameter were uprooted or snapped like twigs.

Continue the hike by retracing your steps to the last trail junction, then turn right. This old road soon comes out into an open meadow in the south branch of the Interior Valley. The meadow gives great views of the most alpine terrain in Arizona, including Doyle, Fremont, Agassiz, and Humphreys Peaks, the four highest of the San Francisco Peaks. Quaking aspen bordering the meadow puts on a beautiful show during October.

Out in the meadow, turn left at another junction in the old road system at mile 4.2. During the summer, a pump house at this junction draws water from a well. Follow the old road down the valley to the east. After the meadow ends and you pass another pump house, you'll meet the trail to Flagstaff Spring where you began the loop portion of the hike. Turn right and retrace your steps past the watershed cabins to return to the Lockett Meadow trailhead.

GOING FARTHER

Options include a 5-mile hike along the old Aubineau Canyon Road to its end in Aubineau Canyon below Humphreys Peak. This would add 10 miles to your hike. A shorter option is to turn right at the first pump house in the south branch of the Interior Valley and hike up the valley on the Inner Basin Trail. This trail continues all the way to the saddle between Fremont and Agassiz Peaks, where it meets the Weatherford Trail.

18. Sunset-Brookbank Loop

RATING	🚶 🚶 🚶 🚶
DISTANCE	5.2-mile loop
HIKING TIME	4 hours
ELEVATION GAIN	750 feet
HIGH POINT	8,763 feet
EFFORT	Moderate Workout
BEST SEASON	Summer, fall
WATER	None
PERMITS/CONTACT	None/Coconino National Forest, (928) 527-3600, www.fs.usda.gov/coconino
MAPS	USGS Sunset Crater West, Humphreys Peak
NOTES	Leashed dogs welcome. Watch for mountain bikes.

THE HIKE

A pleasant walk among the aspens and ponderosa pines of the Dry Lake Hills, this hike also loops through alpine meadows and features views of Flagstaff and the San Francisco Peaks. This is a good hike for fall color.

GETTING THERE

From Flagstaff, drive 3.2 miles north on U.S. 180, turn right on Schultz Pass Road, and drive 5 miles to the Sunset trailhead, on the right. The access roads are dirt and may be impassable during winter or wet weather. Elevation 8,081 feet, GPS coordinates N35°17.121'; W111°37.923'

THE TRAIL

Leave the Sunset trailhead on the Sunset Trail, which first contours just above Schultz Tank, then enters a drainage and starts climbing to the southeast. The well-used and popular trail stays just to the right of the normally dry creek bed, and soon enters a fine mixed forest of ponderosa pine, Douglas fir, and quaking aspen. The trail crosses an old logging road as it nears the head of the drainage, then crosses the drainage to the east and climbs through an alpine meadow to gain the crest of the Dry Lake Hills. This vantage point has views of Mount Elden to the southeast, and the south slopes of the San Francisco Peaks to the north and northwest, including Agassiz, Fremont, and Doyle Peaks.

Snow lingers on Agassiz Peak as seen from the Sunset Trail.

Follow the Sunset Trail to the southwest as it drops off the ridge crest and meets a trail junction at **1.7** miles. Stay right onto the Brookbank Trail (the Sunset Trail goes sharply left) and follow it southwest as it contours back onto the ridge crest and then passes through a saddle. Here

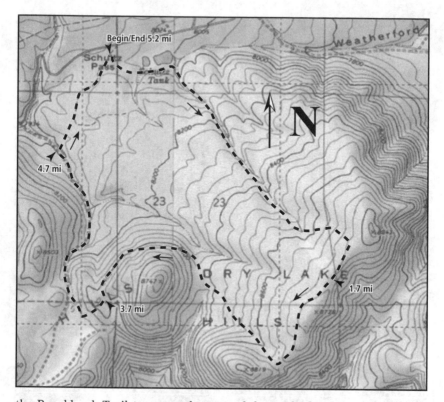

the Brookbank Trail turns northwest and descends through a meadow to another saddle. Now the trail descends around the north side of a densely forested hill and comes out into a saddle on the west side of the hill at **3.7** miles. Turn right on an unmarked trail and descend into a broad meadow. This meadow is one of several that contain shallow seasonal lakes after the spring snowmelt—these are the lakes, dry in late summer and fall, that give the Dry Lake Hills their name.

When the trail comes out into the scattered pines at the edge of the meadow, turn right at another unsigned trail junction. (There are numerous informal trails in this area.) Follow this trail past a stock tank at the north end of the meadow and join an old road. Follow the old road north as it descends the drainage below the stock tank.

At **4.7** miles, leave the old road and turn right on the Schultz Creek Trail. Follow this trail back to the Sunset trailhead.

GOING FARTHER

At the junction with the Brookbank Trail at 1.7 miles, you could turn left to remain on the Sunset Trail. This trail descends through the saddle connecting the Dry Lake Hills to Mount Elden. From here, the Sunset Trail climbs southeast and south toward the summit of Mount Elden, with connections to the Oldham and Mount Elden trails.

Another option is to explore the seasonal lakes and meadows near the 3.7-mile point. You can hike southwest on old roads and visit several meadows and seasonal lakes.

19. Walnut Canyon Rim

RATING	🚶 🚶 🚶
DISTANCE	11.6 miles round-trip
HIKING TIME	6 hours
ELEVATION GAIN	370 feet
HIGH POINT	7,046 feet
EFFORT	Prepare to Perspire
BEST SEASON	Summer, fall
WATER	None
PERMITS/CONTACT	None/Coconino National Forest, (928) 527-3600, www.fs.usda.gov/coconino
MAPS	USGS Flagstaff East
NOTES	Leashed dogs welcome. This trail is shared with mountain bikes and horses. Part of the trail follows old logging roads—pay close attention to the signs to stay on the trail.

THE HIKE

Following part of the Arizona National Scenic Trail, this hike skirts the rim of Walnut Canyon southeast of Flagstaff. This canyon was once inhabited by members of the Sinagua culture, who built small cliff dwellings along the canyon walls, especially downstream in the area of the Walnut Canyon National Monument.

GETTING THERE

From Flagstaff, drive about 8.6 miles east on Interstate 40 and exit at Walnut Canyon Road. Drive 4.4 miles, turn right on Walnut Canyon Road, and drive 1.5 miles to the trailhead, on the left. The access roads are dirt and may be impassable during winter or wet weather. Elevation 6,742 feet, GPS coordinates N35°10.754'; W111°31.786'

THE TRAIL

Follow the Arizona Trail southwest from the trailhead as it meanders along the crest of broad ridges, avoiding a series of side canyons that drain southeast into Walnut Canyon. At 1.9 miles, the trail descends to cross a major side canyon, then climbs south along a ridge. Now the trail

Bright Blue-eyed Mary flowers are found in the ponderosa pine forest in places such as the Arizona Trail along the Walnut Canyon Rim.

turns west briefly before resuming its general southwesterly direction, still staying on top of the broad, pine-forested ridges north of Walnut Canyon.

At **4.0** miles, the trail finally nears the rim of Walnut Canyon itself, where a short spur trail leads south to a viewpoint. From this point the Arizona Trail heads west, closely skirting the north rim of Walnut Canyon. Another junction at **5.8** miles marks Fisher Point. The Arizona Trail

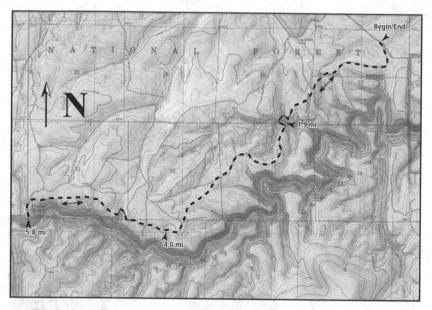

goes right; turn left to walk out onto Fisher Point and enjoy the view of Walnut Canyon. Retrace your steps to return to the trailhead.

GOING FARTHER

From Fisher Point, you can follow the Arizona Trail down into Walnut Canyon, and then follow it south all the way to Mexico if you desire. If that's a bit much, a walk of a mile or two will give you a nice feel for upper Walnut Canyon. A large cliff of Coconino sandstone on the left is a popular spot for rock climbers.

20. Mormon Lake

RATING	🚶 🚶 🚶
DISTANCE	6.5 miles round-trip
HIKING TIME	3 hours
ELEVATION GAIN	Negligible
HIGH POINT	7,200 feet
EFFORT	Easy Walk
BEST SEASON	Spring–fall
WATER	None
PERMITS/CONTACT	None/Coconino National Forest, (928) 527-3600, www.fs.usda.gov/coconino
MAPS	USGS Mormon Lake
NOTES	Leashed dogs welcome, but don't bring a pet if you expect to see wildlife. This nearly level walk follows the remains of the old highway along the edge of the lake. The new highway has been relocated to the top of the bluffs.

THE HIKE

Mormon Lake is the state's largest natural lake, on the rare occasions that it is full. The marshy edges of the lake are a haven for migrating

When full, Mormon Lake is the largest natural lake in Arizona.

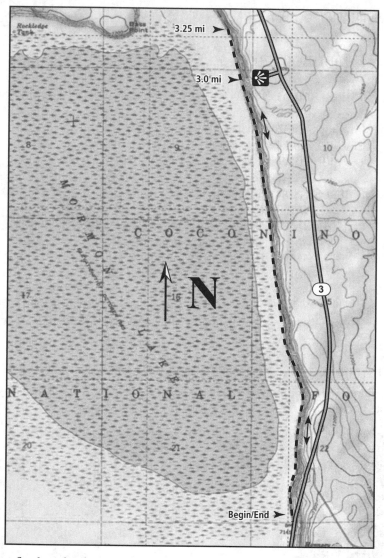

waterfowl and other wildlife, which are best observed early and late in the day.

GETTING THERE

From Flagstaff at the junction of U.S. 180 and Route 66, drive 1.7 miles south on Milton Avenue and turn right on Forest Meadows Street. Go one block, then turn left on Beulah Boulevard. Continue 0.7 mile, then turn left on Lake Mary Road. Drive 24.2 miles, then turn right on an unsigned road at the south end of Mormon Lake. This turnoff is just south of the signed turnoff for Kinnikinick Lake. Elevation 7,150 feet, GPS coordinates N34°55.197'; W111°25.968'

THE TRAIL

Head north through a gate, following the old highway. When Mormon Lake is full, the shoreline is close to the road, but when the lake is lower the water is farther away. In either case, a good pair of binoculars is helpful for observing wildlife. You can follow the old road as far north as you like before turning around. At 3.0 miles the old road passes under a viewpoint located on top of the bluffs off the new highway. A bit farther north, at 3.25 miles, the old highway grade leaves the lakeshore and climbs to meet the new highway. The point where the old road leaves the lakeshore is a good place to turn around.

Creeks in the Mogollon Rim country are a treat for desert hikers.

MOGOLLON RIM COUNTRY

Running more than 200 miles across central Arizona, from west of Sedona to New Mexico, the Rim is a south-facing line of cliffs and bluffs averaging about 2,000 feet high. The Mogollon (pronounced "mug-e-on") Rim marks the southern edge of the Colorado Plateau and the northern edge of the Central Highlands. The area just north of the rim is known as the Mogollon Plateau, and it is heavily forested with a fine mix of ponderosa pine, Douglas fir, and quaking aspen.

There are dozens of canyons cut into the sedimentary rocks along the western and central portion of the Mogollon Rim. Many of these canyons feature permanent streams, a rarity on the generally dry plateau itself. Trails along these shady canyon bottoms are a delight, especially during the warmer months.

Other trails in this section are historic in nature, originally constructed by pioneer ranchers, loggers, and miners attempting to make a living from the resources of the region. Other historic structures remain from the early days of the U.S. Forest Service, when rangers and firefighters were few on the ground and had vast areas to manage, mostly on horseback.

Because of the generally high elevations, the rim country is usually snow-covered from December through March and access roads are impassable. Hikes south of the rim, such as the Sedona area, are usually accessible all year.

MOGOLLON RIM COUNTRY

21. Sycamore Rim Trail

RATING	🚶 🚶 🚶
DISTANCE	10.8-mile loop
HIKING TIME	6 hours
ELEVATION GAIN	800 feet
HIGH POINT	7,230 feet
EFFORT	Moderate Workout
BEST SEASON	Summer, fall
WATER	Seasonal at Dow Spring, Pomeroy Tanks, and Willow Spring
PERMITS/CONTACT	None/Kaibab National Forest, (928) 635-8200, www.fs.usda.gov/kaibab
MAPS	USGS Davenport Hill, Garland Prairie; USFS Sycamore Canyon Wilderness
NOTES	Leashed dogs welcome. You may encounter mountain bikes on the non-wilderness portions of this loop, as well as horses at any time.

THE HIKE

This loop hike wanders through open ponderosa pine forest, climbs over KA Hill, and skirts the rims of Isham Spring, Big Spring, and Sycamore Canyons.

GETTING THERE

From Flagstaff, drive 18 miles west on Interstate 40 then exit at Parks. Turn left, cross the freeway, and drive 9.2 miles on Garland Prairie Road. Turn left on Dow Spring Road and drive 0.7 mile to the Dow Spring trailhead, on the right. The access roads are dirt and may be impassable during winter or wet weather. Elevation 6,732 feet, GPS coordinates N35°09.294'; W111°59.030'

THE TRAIL

Start the loop by hiking west on the Sycamore Rim Trail, which follows upper Sycamore Creek Canyon westward. After passing the site of an old lumber mill, the trail continues west and follows Sycamore Canyon, now very shallow, into a meadow. The trail turns northwest and crosses a

Pines trees growing along a long-abandoned logging railbed.

road at **1.0** mile, then climbs the east slopes of KA Hill. From the 7,287-foot summit, the trail descends along the northwest ridge then turns south and drops down into a drainage. After emerging from the drainage, the trail heads west, crosses another road at **4.9** miles, then turns south along Isham Spring Canyon, which is very shallow at this point.

At **5.9** miles, Isham Spring Canyon meets Big Spring Canyon at a place known locally as Sycamore Falls. Both creek beds plunge over dry falls formed in basalt cliffs, outcrops left over from ancient lava flows. The cliffs in this area are an extremely popular rock-climbing area.

The Sycamore Rim Trail stays on the east rim of Big Spring Canyon downstream of the falls, and heads generally east as the canyon below rapidly grows deeper and more spectacular. At **7.9** miles, the trail meets a spur trail that leads to a trailhead north of Double Tanks. Stay right on the Sycamore Rim Trail as it crosses a point directly north of the confluence of

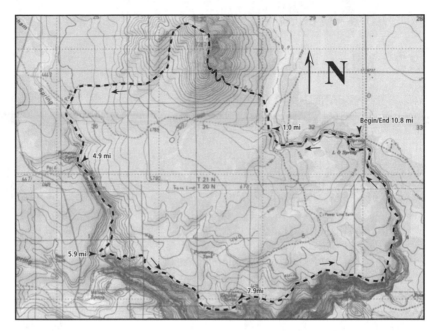

Big Spring and Sycamore Canyons. Now the trail closely follows the north rim of Sycamore Canyon. As the canyon becomes smaller and shallower, the trail turns north, still hugging the rim of the canyon. Finally, at **10.8** miles the trail returns to the Dow Spring trailhead, completing the loop.

Logging was a major industry on the heavily forested Coconino Plateau until the 1990s. Flagstaff was founded largely as a logging town after the Santa Fe Railroad was completed across northern Arizona in 1882 and provided a way to get lumber products to market. Until the 1950s, the primary method for transporting cut timber from the logging sites to the mills in Flagstaff was logging railroads. Temporary tracks were laid on minimally improved roadbeds to reach active harvest areas. When logging was completed in the area, the steel rails were removed for reuse elsewhere. The ties were usually left because it was cheaper to cut new ones—sometimes temporary lumber mills were set up in the forest for the purpose. The site of one such mill is located just west of the Dow Spring trailhead. Today, you can follow the old railroad beds for miles through the forest; they are marked by a thin layer of cinders, rotting ties, and often a line of ponderosa pines that have sprouted from seeds dropped by the rail cars. There are several old logging railroad grades in the section of forest surrounded by the Sycamore Rim Trail.

22. Kelsey-Dorsey Loop

RATING	🚶 🚶 🚶 🚶
DISTANCE	6.5-mile loop
HIKING TIME	4 hours
ELEVATION GAIN	1,120 feet
HIGH POINT	7,000 feet
EFFORT	Moderate Workout
BEST SEASON	Summer, fall
WATER	Seasonal at Kelsey, Babes Hole, and Dorsey Springs
PERMITS/CONTACT	None/Coconino National Forest, (928) 527-3600, www.fs.usda.gov/coconino
MAPS	USGS Sycamore Point; USFS Sycamore Canyon Wilderness
NOTES	Leashed dogs welcome

THE HIKE

A loop hike, this trail dips below the upper rim of Sycamore Canyon, skirts the inner gorge, then returns through open ponderosa pine forest on the southern Coconino Plateau. Along the way, the trail passes three seasonal springs, valuable water sources for wildlife in this land of little surface water.

GETTING THERE

From Flagstaff, drive west on U.S. Route 66 (Business Interstate 40) about 2 miles, then turn left on Woody Mountain Road (Forest Road 231). Continue 13.7 miles, then turn right onto FR 538. Continue 5.3 miles and turn right onto FR 538G. Drive 0.6 mile and turn right at a junction to continue 1.3 miles on FR 538G to the end of the road at the Kelsey trailhead. The access roads are dirt and may be impassable during winter or wet weather. Elevation 6,650 feet, GPS coordinates N35°04.476'; W111°55.785'

THE TRAIL

Follow the Kelsey Trail as it immediately drops off the rim and descends via a couple of short switchbacks. After passing Kelsey Spring, the trail turns south and drops into a shallow drainage. At **1.0** mile, turn left at

Fall color lights up the bed of Sycamore Canyon.

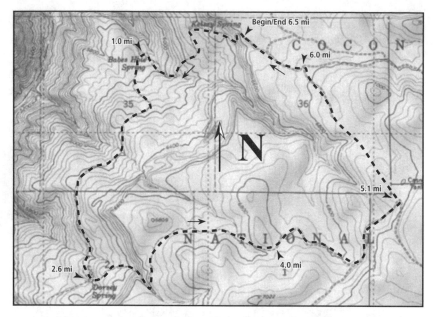

a trail junction just above Babes Hole Spring, and head south on the Dorsey Trail. The Dorsey Trail follows an intermediate bench below the east rim of Sycamore Canyon and there are places with good views of the middle reaches of Sycamore Canyon.

At **2.6** miles, you'll reach Dorsey Spring and another trail junction. Turn left to remain on the Dorsey Trail and follow it up a ravine to the rim. Once at the rim, the Dorsey Trail turns north, passes through a saddle, and heads east through ponderosa pine forest to the Dorsey trailhead at **4.0** miles. Follow the road east to a road junction, turn left, and follow the road north. At another road junction at **5.1** miles, turn left and follow the road northwest (this road is not shown on the topo map). At **6.0** miles, turn left again at a road junction and follow the access road to the Kelsey trailhead, completing the loop hike at **6.5** miles.

GOING FARTHER

The lower Kelsey Trail can be used for a short but interesting side hike to the bed of Sycamore Canyon. Turn right at 1 mile and descend past Babes Hole Spring to Geronimo Spring, which is located near the lower end of Little LO Canyon. Geronimo Spring is the only reliable water source in the upper 43 miles of Sycamore Canyon. The trail ends at the spring, but you can walk a short distance up Little LO Canyon into a nice little narrows, or walk a short distance downstream to Sycamore Canyon itself.

23. Secret Mountain Trail

RATING	🚶 🚶 🚶 🚶
DISTANCE	10.0 miles round-trip
HIKING TIME	5 hours
ELEVATION GAIN	330 feet
HIGH POINT	6,666 feet
EFFORT	Moderate Workout
BEST SEASON	Summer, fall
WATER	None
PERMITS/CONTACT	None/Coconino National Forest, (928) 527-3600, www.fs.usda.gov/coconino
MAPS	USGS Loy Butte, Wilson Mountain
NOTES	Leashed dogs welcome

THE HIKE

This hike leads to several spectacular viewpoints overlooking the red rock canyons above Sedona.

GETTING THERE

From Flagstaff, drive west on U.S. Route 66 (Business Interstate 40) about 2 miles, then turn left on Woody Mountain Road (Forest Road 231). Continue 13.7 miles and turn right at Phone Booth Tank onto FR 538. Continue 11.6 miles to the end of the road at Secret Mountain trailhead. The access roads are dirt and may be impassable during winter or wet weather. Elevation 6,532 feet, GPS coordinates N34°58.813'; W111°54.086'

THE TRAIL

From the trailhead, follow the Secret Mountain Trail off the edge of the Mogollon Rim and down to a saddle and trail junction at 0.4 mile, located at the heads of Secret and Loy Canyons. Stay left on the Secret Mountain Trail and follow it south onto the north rim of Secret Mountain. This is the only trail access to the broad top of Secret Mountain, which is almost completely surrounded by sheer cliffs. The trail heads south and crosses a drainage at the ruins of Secret Cabin, a structure apparently once used by U.S. Forest Service firefighters.

Claret cup cactus, found in the ponderosa pine forests, is easily overlooked until it breaks out in brilliant red flowers.

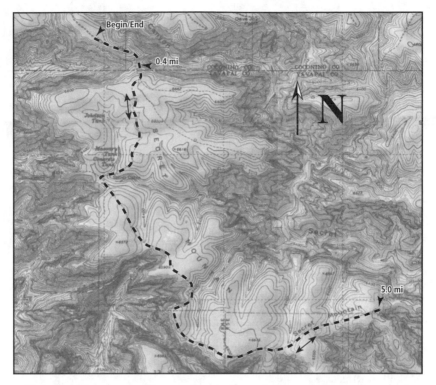

Now heading generally southeast through the open ponderosa pine forest, the Secret Mountain Trail loosely skirts the west rim of Secret Mountain, then heads east along the south rim. This portion of the trail has some fine views of the red rock country. The trail finally ends at the southeast corner of Secret Mountain, at an overlook above Secret and Long Canyons.

GOING FARTHER
See the Loy Canyon Trail (hike #24 in this guide) for the possibility of an extended hike from the saddle between the Mogollon Rim and Secret Mountain.

24. Loy Canyon Trail

RATING	🚶 🚶 🚶 🚶
DISTANCE	9.6 miles round-trip
HIKING TIME	6 hours
ELEVATION GAIN	1,875 feet
HIGH POINT	6,560 feet
EFFORT	Moderate Workout
BEST SEASON	Fall–spring
WATER	None
PERMITS/CONTACT	None/Coconino National Forest, (928) 527-3600, www.fs.usda.gov/coconino
MAPS	USGS Loy Butte
NOTES	Leashed dogs welcome

THE HIKE

This hike follows a red rock canyon to its head at the southern edge of the Colorado Plateau, on the Mogollon Rim. The Loy Canyon Trail is one of a few trails that connect the red rock country around Sedona with the Mogollon Rim.

GETTING THERE

From Sedona, drive west on AZ 89A, then turn right onto Dry Creek Road at a traffic light. Drive 2.8 miles and stay left onto Boynton Canyon Road. Continue 1.6 miles, then turn left onto Forest Road 152C. After 3 miles, turn right onto FR 525. Continue 3.7 miles to the Loy Canyon trailhead. The access roads are dirt and may be impassable during winter or wet weather. Elevation 4,688 feet, GPS coordinates N34°56.095'; W111°55.630'

THE TRAIL

From the trailhead, the Loy Canyon Trail first skirts around private property owned by the Hancock Ranch, then heads north up the dry bed of Sycamore Canyon. Loy Butte, a massive formation in the rounded red rocks of the Schnebly Hill Formation, towers above the trail to the west. Other red rock formations appear as you proceed up the canyon.

Yarrow is often present during a wet summer monsoon.

Although many of the horizontal layers of sedimentary rock persist throughout the vast Colorado Plateau, the Schnebly Hill Formation is not one of them. This rock layer disappears before rocks at this depth are again exposed at the eastern end of the Grand Canyon.

As you continue upstream, Loy Canyon narrows and turns north-northeast. A buff-colored layer of the Coconino sandstone forms massive cliffs in the upper portions of Loy Canyon. Formed in a Sahara-like dune field that once covered much of what is now northern Arizona, the

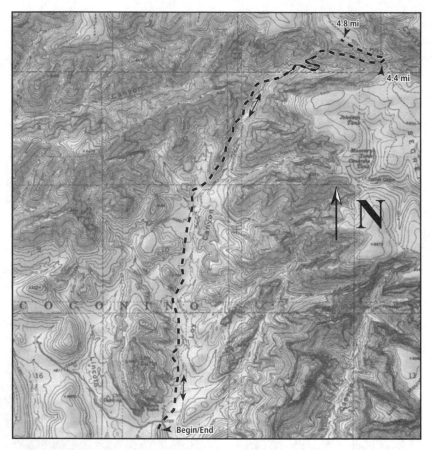

Coconino sandstone also forms sheer cliffs in the central and eastern Grand Canyon.

A couple of switchbacks lead the trail out of the bed of Loy Canyon for the ascent of the head of the canyon. The trail ends in a saddle at the junction with the Secret Mountain Trail at **4.4** miles. Turn left and follow the Secret Mountain Trail 0.4 mile to the Mogollon Rim, the Secret Mountain trailhead, and the turnaround point.

GOING FARTHER
You can do a long side hike of 9.2 miles round-trip by using the Secret Mountain Trail (hike #23 in this guide).

25. Secret Canyon

RATING	𝐀 𝐀 𝐀 𝐀 𝐀
DISTANCE	7.8 miles round-trip
HIKING TIME	5 hours
ELEVATION GAIN	430 feet
HIGH POINT	5,092 feet
EFFORT	Moderate Workout
BEST SEASON	Spring, fall
WATER	Seasonal in upper Secret Canyon
PERMITS/CONTACT	None/Coconino National Forest, (928) 527-3600, www.fs.usda.gov/coconino
MAPS	USGS Wilson Mountain
NOTES	Leashed dogs welcome

THE HIKE

Because this hike is longer than most in the Red Rock/Sedona area, it is a good place to avoid the crowds. It is also very pretty during the fall when the colors are changing in the upper canyon.

GETTING THERE

From Sedona, drive west on AZ 89A and turn right on Dry Creek Road at a traffic light. Continue 2 miles, then turn right on Forest Road 152. Continue 3.2 miles to the Secret Canyon trailhead. Parking is limited. The access roads are dirt and may be impassable during winter or wet weather. Elevation 4,663 feet, GPS coordinates N34°55.781'; W111°48.385'

THE TRAIL

The Secret Canyon Trail starts out by immediately crossing aptly named Dry Creek (if the creek is running, it's probably flooding and you should not attempt to cross it). After the crossing, follow the trail along the bed of Secret Canyon. The trail crosses the dry creek bed several times, but finally climbs out on the right side and stays there. After passing through a small clearing at the 2.0-mile point, the trail turns west and heads into the middle section of Secret Canyon. The walls of the canyon close in and soon tower above the trail. After the trail crosses the creek again, it generally stays on the south side just above the bed. Fall color along this

The Dry Creek Basin has seven major side canyons, including Secret Canyon.

section is provided by some of the deciduous trees that are found along many streamsides in Arizona—Arizona ash and Arizona bigtooth maple. Another plant that changes color is poison ivy, which becomes scarlet during the fall. Usually no more than 1 or 2 feet tall, poison ivy grows along many streamsides at intermediate elevations in Arizona. Poison ivy is readily identified by its glossy leaves that grow in groups of three.

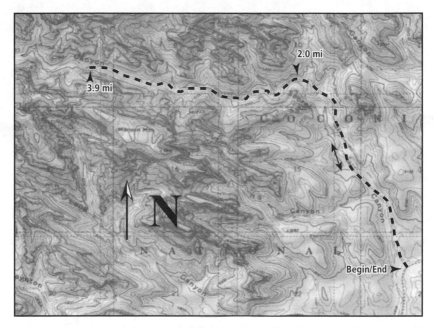

At approximately the **3.9**-mile point the trail fades away. Turn around here unless you are prepared for canyoneering and bushwhacking.

GOING FARTHER

Just before reaching the clearing at 2.0 miles, an obscure trail comes in from the right. This trail may be followed over a saddle to the Bear Sign Canyon Trail (hike #26 in this guide), which in turn can be followed right (downstream) to the Dry Creek trailhead. Then walk a mile down Dry Creek Road to return to the Secret Canyon trailhead.

26. Bear Sign Canyon

RATING	🚶 🚶 🚶 🚶
DISTANCE	4.5 miles round-trip
HIKING TIME	3 hours
ELEVATION GAIN	390 feet
HIGH POINT	5,160 feet
EFFORT	Easy Walk
BEST SEASON	Spring, fall
WATER	None
PERMITS/CONTACT	None/Coconino National Forest, (928) 527-3600, www.fs.usda.gov/coconino
MAPS	USGS Wilson Mountain
NOTES	Leashed dogs welcome

THE HIKE
An easy hike up one of the many canyons in the Dry Creek Basin, this walk nevertheless takes you deep into a scenic red rock canyon.

GETTING THERE
From Sedona, drive west on AZ 89A and turn right on Dry Creek Road at a traffic light. Continue 2 miles and turn right on Forest Road 152. Continue 4 miles to the Dry Creek trailhead at the end of the road. The access roads are dirt and may be impassable during winter or wet weather. Elevation 4,792 feet, GPS coordinates N34°56.215'; W111°47.702'

Fair weather clouds float in the sky above the red rock country near Sedona.

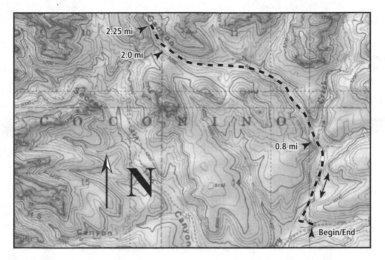

THE TRAIL

Two trails depart from the Dry Creek trailhead—this hike uses the left-hand one, Dry Creek Trail, to start off. Follow the trail up Dry Creek, which is normally dry, through a mixed woodland of pinyon pine, juniper, and Arizona cypress. Juniper trees and pinyon pines grow about 10 to 15 feet high and form a woodland in miniature that covers vast areas of the Colorado Plateau. Arizona cypress, in contrast, is only found in central Arizona. It's easy to spot because of its straight trunk with reddish, curly bark.

At **0.8** mile, the canyons fork at a trail junction. Turn left onto Bear Sign Canyon Trail and follow this good, easy trail up Bear Sign Canyon. At about **2.0** miles, a trail forks left; stay right and continue up Bear Sign Canyon. As you proceed, the trail fades out—the exact point depends on recent use, but many hikers turn around at about **2.25** miles. Like many of the canyons in the Dry Creek area, the official, maintained trail goes partway up the canyon and hikers informally extend the trail to the point where dry falls or brush make the going difficult.

GOING FARTHER

See the Secret Canyon Trail (hike #25 in this guide) for a loop hike using the side trail at 2.0 miles. This trail climbs over a red rock saddle and joins the Secret Canyon Trail at about its 2-mile point. You could then turn left and follow the Secret Canyon Trail downstream to the Secret Canyon trailhead. Now turn left and walk 1 mile up the Dry Creek Road to the Dry Creek trailhead.

27. Thomas Point Trail

RATING	🚶 🚶 🚶 🚶
DISTANCE	2.6 miles round-trip
HIKING TIME	2 hours
ELEVATION GAIN	970 feet
HIGH POINT	6,275 feet
EFFORT	Moderate Workout
BEST SEASON	Spring–fall
WATER	None
PERMITS/CONTACT	Red Rock Pass required/Coconino National Forest, (928) 527-3600, www.fs.usda.gov/coconino
MAPS	USGS Munds Park
NOTES	Leashed dogs welcome

THE HIKE

This is a good hike for those who wish to avoid the crowds on the West Fork Trail on the opposite side of Oak Creek Canyon. It offers an overview of the West Fork of Oak Creek from the east rim of Oak Creek Canyon.

GETTING THERE

From Sedona, drive 10.6 miles north on AZ 89A to the West Fork trailhead on the left. This is a fee parking area in addition to the Red Rock Pass. Elevation 5,307 feet, GPS coordinates N34°59.286'; W111°44.703'

THE TRAIL

From the West Fork parking lot, walk about 0.2 mile south on a trail paralleling the highway, then cross the highway to the start of the Thomas Point Trail, which is signed (there is no parking along the highway—you must park in the West Fork parking lot).

The trail climbs through the open ponderosa pine forest above the busy highway, then swings around onto a much drier, south-facing slope. Several switchbacks lead to a saddle at 1.2 miles, and from here the trail climbs just bit more to end at the east rim of Oak Creek Canyon at 1.3 miles. You can easily walk a hundred yards along the rim either to the north or south to get views of Oak Creek Canyon.

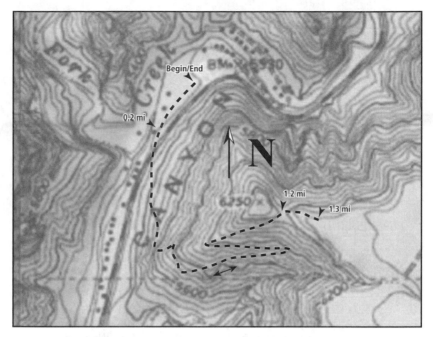

Like most of the trails built from Oak Creek to the rim of Oak Creek Canyon, the Thomas Point Trail was constructed by an early settler as a route to Flagstaff. Because it was on the transcontinental Santa Fe Railroad, Flagstaff was the nearest point of supply for homesteads and ranches in the area. A settler would lead a pack string up a trail to the east rim of Oak Creek. From that point they could head north through the forest to the growing city. Some people left a wagon at the rim so they could hitch up their team and haul a larger load of goods to sell in Flagstaff, then bring back more supplies in return. So, when you're complaining about the slow traffic on AZ 89A through Oak Creek, remember that the pioneers had to make an all-day trip to reach Flagstaff.

GOING FARTHER

Another viewpoint can be reached from the saddle just before the end of the trail. Leave the trail and walk west about 0.1 mile onto the top of the rocky hill. This vantage point offers a panoramic overview of the confluence of the wilderness West Fork and busy Oak Creek Canyon.

28. West Fork Trail

RATING	🚶 🚶 🚶 🚶
DISTANCE	6.0 miles round-trip
HIKING TIME	3 hours
ELEVATION GAIN	220 feet
HIGH POINT	5,500 feet
EFFORT	Easy Walk
BEST SEASON	Spring–fall
WATER	West Fork
PERMITS/CONTACT	Red Rock Pass required/Coconino National Forest, (928) 527-3600, www.fs.usda.gov/coconino
MAPS	USGS Munds Park, Wilson Mountain, Dutton Hill. The trail is not shown on the topo maps.
NOTES	Leashed dogs permitted but not advisable due to poison ivy. Though dogs don't react to poison ivy, they can get the poisonous sap on you. Camping is not allowed in the lower 6 miles of the West Fork due to heavy use.

THE HIKE

This hike is rated four only because of the crowds. Scenery-wise it is a strong five—definitely one of the most spectacular easy hikes in Arizona. The trail gently wanders through deep, cool pine and fir forest, crossing a small permanent stream, while red and white sandstone cliffs and buttresses tower hundreds of feet overhead.

GETTING THERE

From Sedona, drive 10.6 miles north on AZ 89A to the West Fork trailhead on the left. There is a fee for the parking area, in addition to the Red Rock Pass. Elevation 5,307 feet, GPS coordinates N34°59.286'; W111°44.703'

THE TRAIL

Follow the West Fork Trail across the bridge over Oak Creek, then downstream along the right bank of the creek. After 0.2 mile, the trail turns right and heads up the West Fork. For the next 2.8 miles, the trail crosses

Hikers enjoying fall foliage along the West Fork Trail.

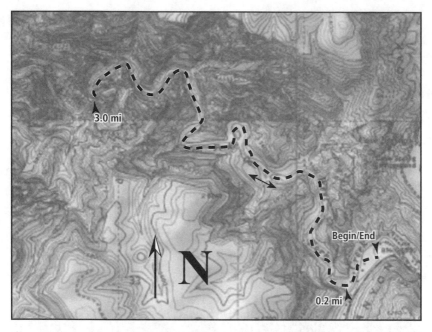

the small creek numerous times, alternating with pleasant pine flats, and
the walking is easy. At about **3.0** miles, the canyon floor narrows significantly and the trail ends. This is the turnaround point for your hike.
The first of many deep pools floods the canyon from wall to wall and
canyoneering skills are needed to travel farther upstream.

29. AB Young Trail

RATING	🚶 🚶 🚶 🚶
DISTANCE	4.0 miles round-trip
HIKING TIME	3 hours
ELEVATION GAIN	1,950 feet
HIGH POINT	7,195 feet
EFFORT	Moderate Workout
BEST SEASON	Spring–fall
WATER	None
PERMITS/CONTACT	Red Rock Pass required/Coconino National Forest, (928) 527-3600, www.fs.usda.gov/coconino
MAPS	USGS Wilson Mountain
NOTES	Leashed dogs welcome

THE HIKE
Of all the trails that lead out of Oak Creek Canyon, this is the only one that climbs to the west rim.

GETTING THERE
From Sedona, drive 9 miles north on AZ 89A and park near the entrance to Bootlegger Picnic Area. There is no signed trailhead—do not block

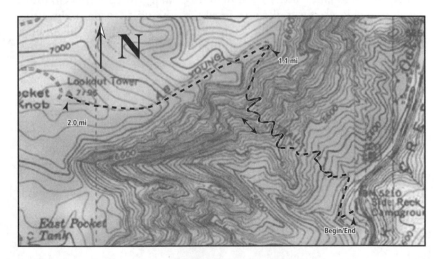

Agave, or century plant, is common on the slopes of Oak Creek Canyon.

the entrance to the picnic area. Elevation 5,256 feet, GPS coordinates N34°58.206'; W111°45.032'

THE TRAIL

Cross Oak Creek at the downstream end of the picnic area and look for an old trail along the west side of the creek. Follow this trail to the right, upstream. Within a few yards the AB Young Trail forks left and immediately starts to climb away from the creek. Many switchbacks climb the brushy hillside as the trail seeks breaks in the cliffs to gain elevation. Although the trail is hot in the summer and has little shade, the absence of deep forest definitely improves the view down Oak Creek Canyon. After 1.1 miles, the AB Young Trail finally reaches the west rim of Oak Creek. It now turns southwest and follows the rim for about 0.5 mile before turning west. The trail ends at East Pocket Lookout, a fire tower staffed by the U.S. Forest Service during the summer fire season. Ask permission from the lookout before climbing the stairs.

Unlike the trails on the east side of Oak Creek, the AB Young Trail was built primarily for access to summer grazing pastures on the plateau west of the canyon, rather than as a route to Flagstaff. Any horse or wagon trip to Flagstaff from East Pocket Knob would have had to make a major detour around the head of the West Fork of Oak Creek.

30. Wilson Mountain Trail

RATING	🚶 🚶 🚶 🚶
DISTANCE	7.1 miles round-trip
HIKING TIME	5 hours
ELEVATION GAIN	2,480 feet
HIGH POINT	6,980 feet
EFFORT	Prepare to Perspire
BEST SEASON	Spring–fall
WATER	None
PERMITS/CONTACT	Red Rock Pass required/Coconino National Forest, (928) 527-3600, www.fs.usda.gov/coconino
MAPS	USGS Wilson Mountain
NOTES	Leashed dogs welcome

THE HIKE

Your reward for making the steep climb to the mesa-like top of Wilson Mountain is one of the best views of Sedona, lower Oak Creek, and the red rock country.

GETTING THERE

From Sedona, drive 1.9 miles north on AZ 89A, cross Midgely Bridge, and park on the left. Elevation 4,532 feet, GPS coordinates N34°53.139'; W111°44.493'

THE TRAIL

Walk to the north end of the parking lot and follow the Wilson Mountain Trail along the east side of Wilson Canyon. The trail soon starts to climb via a series of broad switchbacks. As you gain elevation you also gain a wider view of the lower end of Oak Creek Canyon. At the top of this climb the Wilson Mountain Trail reaches the south rim of a small sloping plateau, the First Bench of Wilson Mountain. As you continue northwest up the slope, you'll meet the North Wilson Mountain Trail at mile **2.4**. Turn left to remain on the Wilson Mountain Trail. The trail climbs up a ravine to reach a saddle on the summit plateau at **3.0** miles. This is the end of the official trail but not the end of your hike.

Looking north over Bear Wallow Canyon and Wilson Mountain.

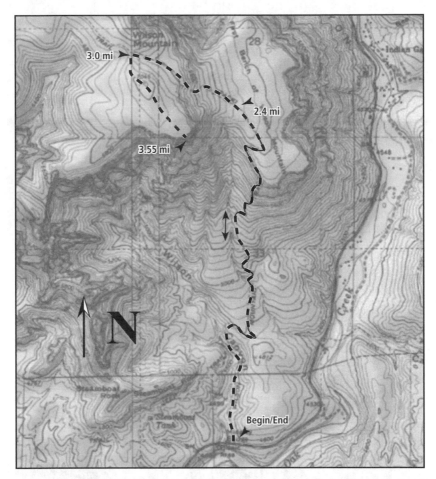

The summit of Wilson Mountain is a rock knob just to the north of the saddle. Although the view was improved by the forest fire that killed many of the trees on Wilson Mountain, a still better view can be found by heading south and then southeast (left) from the saddle, following an informal trail to a viewpoint at the southeast edge of the mesa. This spot, on the edge of a high basalt cliff, offers a fine panoramic view of Sedona, the lower end of Oak Creek Canyon, and much of the red rock country.

The fire that burned all of Wilson Mountain during the summer of 2006 was started by an illegal campfire below the west side of the mountain. Fire danger was extreme and the wildfire quickly burned most of the ponderosa pine and Douglas fir on the mountain.

31. Huckaby Trail

RATING	🚶 🚶 🚶 🚶
DISTANCE	4.3 miles round-trip
HIKING TIME	2 hours
ELEVATION GAIN	200 feet
HIGH POINT	4,500 feet
EFFORT	Easy Walk
BEST SEASON	Year-round
WATER	Oak Creek
PERMITS/CONTACT	None/Coconino National Forest, (928) 527-3600, www.fs.usda.gov/coconino
MAPS	USGS Munds Mountain, Wilson Mountain
NOTES	Leashed dogs welcome

THE HIKE

The Huckaby Trail is one of the few that follow Oak Creek for any distance. The walk along the creek is a rare chance to enjoy the riparian (streamside) habitat, a valuable resource in this country of few perennial streams.

Steamboat Mountain and Wilson Mountain as seen from the Huckaby Trail.

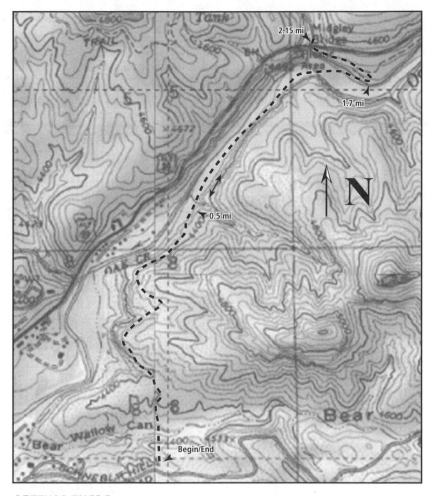

GETTING THERE

From Sedona at the junction of AZ 89A and AZ 179, drive 0.4 mile
south on AZ 179 and turn left on Schnebly Hill Road. Continue 0.7 mile
and park on the left. Elevation 4,404 feet, GPS coordinates N34°51.980';
W111°44.992'

THE TRAIL

Follow the Huckaby Trail north across the dry bed of Bear Wallow Canyon, then across the slope on the east side of Oak Creek Canyon. After
about **0.5** mile the trail takes advantage of a break in the sandstone cliffs

to descend to Oak Creek, which meanders back and forth across a broad floodplain at the bottom of the canyon. Follow the trail upstream to the northeast. It is easy to reach the bank of Oak Creek itself from several places along the trail, and since the access is by trail rather than car the creek is much less crowded than it is upstream.

When Oak Creek makes a turn to the east at **1.7** miles, the trail crosses the creek and climbs the north side of the canyon to end at a viewpoint below Midgley Bridge on AZ 89A.

GOING FARTHER

A major extension of your hike is possible by continuing up the Wilson Mountain Trail from the Midgley Bridge viewpoint. To do this, cross under the bridge on a trail and follow it up to the parking lot at the Wilson Mountain trailhead. See the Wilson Mountain Trail (hike #30 in this guide).

32. Munds Mountain Trail

RATING	🚶 🚶 🚶 🚶
DISTANCE	5.6 miles round-trip
HIKING TIME	4 hours
ELEVATION GAIN	1,200 feet
HIGH POINT	6,782 feet
EFFORT	Moderate Workout
BEST SEASON	Spring–fall
WATER	None
PERMITS/CONTACT	None/Coconino National Forest, (928) 527-3600, www.fs.usda.gov/coconino
MAPS	USGS Munds Park, Munds Mountain
NOTES	Leashed dogs welcome

THE HIKE

This hike at the head of Bear Wallow Canyon follows parts of a historic road and ends up at the top of Munds Mountain, a high mesa just east of Sedona.

GETTING THERE

From Sedona at the junction of AZ 89A and AZ 179, drive 0.4 mile south on AZ 179 and turn left on Schnebly Hill Road. Continue 5.1 miles and park on the left where the road passes through a small saddle. The access roads are dirt and may be impassable during winter or wet weather. Elevation 5,616 feet, GPS coordinates N34°52.942'; W111°42.655'

THE TRAIL

Walk across the Schnebly Hill Road and look for a trail climbing the hillside above and just south of the saddle. Hike up this trail, which is actually an old road, as it gains elevation in a single switchback before setting off to the south. This section of the trail is the original route of the Schnebly Hill Road, the first road built from the Sedona/Oak Creek area to the Coconino Plateau above. This was the only road directly connecting Sedona and Flagstaff until the present highway was built up Oak Creek Canyon in the 1950s.

Camping on the red rocks below the Munds Mountain Trail.

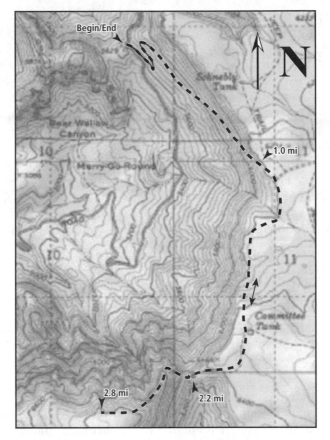

At **1.0** mile, the old road reaches the rim and veers away to the east. Stay right, along the rim, and continue the hike on the Munds Mountain Trail, now a foot trail. The trail loosely follows the rim above Bear Wallow Canyon until it descends to a saddle at **2.2** miles. Here, the Jacks Canyon Trail heads south down Jacks Canyon, but you should continue straight ahead on the Munds Mountain Trail, which climbs up the northeast ridge of Munds Mountain to reach the broad summit plateau. Your hike ends here, overlooking Bear Wallow Canyon from above the imposing cliffs on the north face of Munds Mountain. The trail wanders south from here, and you can walk to the highest point of the mountain (labeled "6834" on the topo map), but the view is not all that good from the gently rounded, brushy summit.

33. Bell Trail

RATING	🚶 🚶 🚶 🚶 🚶
DISTANCE	6.7 miles round-trip
HIKING TIME	4 hours
ELEVATION GAIN	410 feet
HIGH POINT	4,250 feet
EFFORT	Easy Walk
BEST SEASON	Spring–fall
WATER	Wet Beaver Creek
PERMITS/CONTACT	None/Coconino National Forest, (928) 527-3600, www.fs.usda.gov/coconino
MAPS	USGS Casner Butte
NOTES	Leashed dogs welcome

THE HIKE
Because this trail follows alongside Wet Beaver Creek, it is a very popular hike during warm weather when people take advantage of the natural swimming holes.

GETTING THERE
From Interstate 17 and AZ 179 north of Camp Verde, go 2.3 miles east on Forest Road 618 and turn left into the Wet Beaver Creek trailhead. Elevation 3,873 feet, GPS coordinates N34°40.446'; W111°42.865'

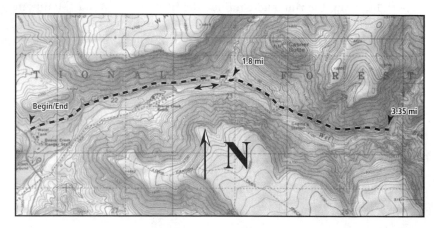

Bright red cactus flowers appear in early summer along the Bell Trail.

THE TRAIL

The Bell Trail starts out as an old road, now closed, that heads east into the deep canyon cut into the Mogollon Rim by Wet Beaver Creek. After about **1.0** mile you'll pass by Beaver Creek Ranch, which is located across the creek. At **1.8** miles a major side canyon comes in from the left, then the Apache Maid Trail forks left. Stay right on the Bell Trail. The old road ends and the trail becomes a foot trail and descends near the creek. Numerous short side trails lead down to the creek. Your hike ends at **3.35** miles where a major side canyon comes in from the right and the Bell Trail crosses Wet Beaver Creek to climb out of the canyon. This is a pleasant spot to enjoy a leisurely lunch before starting the hike back.

GOING FARTHER
Both the Apache Maid and Bell Trails lead out of the canyon onto the plateau above. The climb to the rim is worth doing on each trail for the view.

34. West Clear Creek

RATING	🚶 🚶 🚶 🚶 🚶
DISTANCE	10.8 miles round-trip
HIKING TIME	6 hours
ELEVATION GAIN	450 feet
HIGH POINT	4,045 feet
EFFORT	Moderate Workout
BEST SEASON	Spring–fall
WATER	West Clear Creek
PERMITS/CONTACT	None/Coconino National Forest, (928) 527-3600, www.fs.usda.gov/coconino
MAPS	USGS Walker Mountain, Buckhorn Mountain
NOTES	Leashed dogs welcome

THE HIKE

This is an open-ended walk up the lower end of West Clear Creek. You can continue the hike many miles beyond the endpoint of the hike described here, but be prepared to swim pools and float your gear.

GETTING THERE

From Interstate 17 at Camp Verde, drive 12.2 miles east on AZ 260 and turn left on Forest Road 618. Continue 2.2 miles, then turn right on Bull Pen Road and drive 2.8 miles to the end of the road. The access roads are dirt and may be impassable during winter or wet weather. Elevation 3,587 feet, GPS coordinates N34°32.403'; W111°42.402'

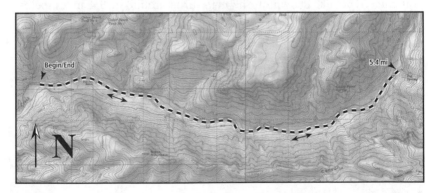

West Clear Creek cascades the length of West Clear Creek Road.

THE TRAIL

From the parking area, the trail heads east across a flat well away from the creek. It passes the remains of the Bull Pen Ranch and a major side canyon coming in from the north before it finally descends to the creek. Above this point, the trail crosses West Clear Creek numerous times, which can be difficult or impossible during spring runoff. Hike upstream as far as you like or have time for, then turn around and return the way you came. The hike shown on the map turns around at **5.4** miles, below Big Spring.

GOING FARTHER

It is possible to hike the entire length of West Clear Creek and exit via the Tramway or Maxwell Trails to the north rim. These trails enter West Clear Creek below the confluence of Clover and Willow Creeks. As mentioned before, this trek takes several days and requires canyoneering skills to swim pools and float your gear.

35. Fossil Springs Trail

RATING	🚶 🚶 🚶 🚶
DISTANCE	7.2 miles round-trip
HIKING TIME	5 hours
ELEVATION GAIN	1,390 feet
HIGH POINT	5,660 feet
EFFORT	Moderate Workout
BEST SEASON	Spring-fall
WATER	Fossil Creek
PERMITS/CONTACT	None/Coconino National Forest, (928) 527-3600, www.fs.usda.gov/coconino
MAPS	USGS Strawberry
NOTES	Leashed dogs welcome

THE HIKE

This hike leads to Fossil Creek, a permanent stream fed by warm springs, and the site of a historic hydroelectric project.

GETTING THERE

From Strawberry on AZ 87, go west 4.7 miles on Fossil Creek Road and turn right. Drive 0.4 mile to the trailhead at the end of the road. The access

From the air, Fossil Creek Canyon cuts into the edge of the Colorado Plateau at the Mogollon Rim.

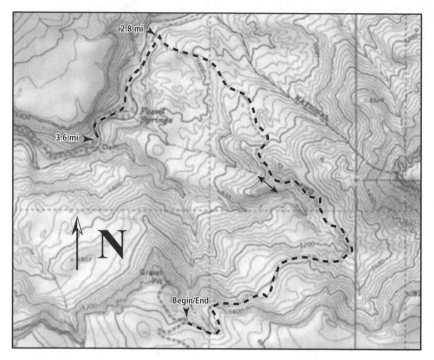

roads are dirt and may be impassable during winter or wet weather. Elevation 5,568 feet, GPS coordinates N34°24.529'; W111°34.124'

THE TRAIL

The Fossil Springs Trail heads east and descends below the south rim of the canyon. After crossing a drainage below Nash Point, the trail turns northwest and works its way to a ridge, which it then follows down to Fossil Creek at 2.8 miles. The creek usually has some flow where the trail meets and crosses it, but less than 0.4 mile downstream you'll reach Fossil Springs, a series of large, warm springs that pour into the right bank of the creek, greatly adding to the flow. Just below the springs, the trail ends at a small dam and the remains of a diversion system.

This project was built in 1912 to supply power to Payson and Phoenix. Water was diverted into a flume and pipeline system and powered two hydroelectric turbines, one a few miles downstream and the other at the Verde River. The power plants were decommissioned in 2005, and the full natural flow returned to lower Fossil Creek. The owner of the power system, Arizona Public Service, decided that the tiny amount of power generated was not worth the environmental cost to lower Fossil Creek.

With the full flow restored, lower Fossil Creek is once again becoming a major habitat for wildlife and the travertine pools and falls are being rebuilt by the mineralized waters of the creek.

GOING FARTHER
It is possible to turn right instead of left when the trail first meets Fossil Creek, and explore upper Fossil Creek as far as you desire. This portion of Fossil Creek sees far fewer hikers than the Fossil Springs and lower Fossil Creek areas, but you must be prepared to follow faint trails and hike cross-country.

36. Kinder Crossing Trail

RATING	🚶 🚶 🚶 🚶
DISTANCE	2.9 miles round-trip
HIKING TIME	2 hours
ELEVATION GAIN	625 feet
HIGH POINT	7,070 feet
EFFORT	Easy Walk
BEST SEASON	Spring–fall
WATER	East Clear Creek
PERMITS/CONTACT	None/Coconino National Forest, (928) 527-3600, www.fs.usda.gov/coconino
MAPS	USGS Blue Ridge Reservoir
NOTES	Leashed dogs welcome

THE HIKE

This is a short walk along a historic trail, the remains of an extensive foot-and-pack transportation system that enabled the early settlers and ranchers to travel the Mogollon Rim country.

GETTING THERE

From Clints Well on AZ 87 north of Payson, drive north 9 miles on AZ 87. Turn right on Forest Road 95. Continue 4.2 miles and turn left. Continue 0.6 mile to the Kinder trailhead at the end of the road. The access roads are dirt and may be impassable during winter or wet weather. Elevation 7,076 feet, GPS coordinates N34°34.010'; W111°09.440'

THE TRAIL

The Kinder Crossing Trail descends a ridge to East Clear Creek, a permanent stream. It crosses the creek at **0.9** miles and then climbs to the east rim above Yaeger Canyon.

The deep canyons running north from the Mogollon Rim made travel difficult for the pioneers on the forested ridges. Trails took advantage of breaks in the cliffs to cross the canyons, places that soon became known as "crossings." Some, such as Jones Crossing, are now traversed by graded and maintained National Forest roads, while others, such as Kinder Crossing, still can be crossed only by trail. Most of the trails that

Scarlet penstemon adds a splash of color to the pine forest near Kinder Crossing.

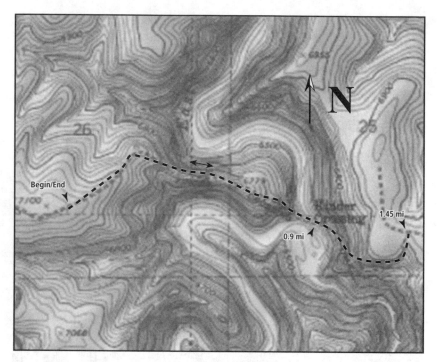

once traversed the forested ridges are gone, wiped out by modern forest roads and logging. A few remain—see Cabin Loop (hike #37 in this guide) for a hike on some of these trails.

GOING FARTHER

It is possible to hike for miles either up- or downstream from the point where Kinder Crossing Trail crosses East Clear Creek. Be prepared to wade the creek frequently.

37. Cabin Loop

RATING	🚶 🚶 🚶 🚶
DISTANCE	17.8-mile loop
HIKING TIME	10 hours or 2 days
ELEVATION GAIN	720 feet
HIGH POINT	7,685 feet
EFFORT	Prepare to Perspire
BEST SEASON	Summer, fall
WATER	Barbershop Canyon, McClintock Spring, Dane Canyon, Dane Spring, McFarland Spring, and Aspen Spring; seasonal at Coyote Spring and Barbershop Spring
PERMITS/CONTACT	None/Coconino National Forest, (928) 527-3600, www.fs.usda.gov/coconino
MAPS	USGS Blue Ridge Reservoir, Dane Canyon
NOTES	Leashed dogs welcome. You may encounter horses and mountain bikes. Parts of these trails follow two-track roads and then leave the road as a foot trail. Pay careful attention to the tree blazes. Camping is limited in the canyon bottoms—plan to pick up water at a creek or spring and then dry camp on the flat ridges between canyons. The Cabin Loop trails are not shown on the topo maps.

THE HIKE

Set in the vast pine forests of the Mogollon Plateau north of the Mogollon Rim, this hike uses a series of restored historic trails collectively known as the Cabin Loop. As described, the hike starts and ends at one of the three historic cabins, while a second cabin is just a short side hike away.

GETTING THERE

From Clints Well on AZ 87 north of Payson, drive north 9 miles on AZ 87. Turn right on Forest Road 95. Continue 11.1 miles and turn left on FR 139A. After 0.1 mile, park where the Fred Haught Trail crosses the road. The access roads are dirt and may be impassable during winter or wet weather. Elevation 7,033 feet, GPS coordinates N34°30.561'; W111°11.794'

Setting out for a hike on the U-Bar Trail at Pinchot Cabin.

THE TRAIL

Follow the old road down to Pinchot Cabin and a trail junction at 0.3 mile. Start the loop on the U-Bar Trail next to the cabin. Follow the U-Bar Trail onto a ridge to the east of the cabin, then southeast onto a broad ridge. The trail crosses Dick Hart Draw and then a maintained forest road before dropping down to cross Barbershop Canyon near the confluence with Merritt Draw at 3.2 miles.

In general, these old trails disappeared or were replaced by roads on the broad ridges. Only the canyon crossings survived. In restoring the trails, the U.S. Forest Service followed two-track roads where appropriate, and blazed a route along the known trails where there were no roads. When first reopened, the Cabin Loop Trails were mostly a blazed route on the ridges with no visible trail tread, but have since become popular enough so that an actual trail now exists. Watch for original construction where the trails cross major canyons, such as Barbershop and Dane Canyons.

After climbing out of Barbershop Canyon, the U-Bar Trail crosses McClintock Ridge and then descends slightly to pass McClintock Spring.

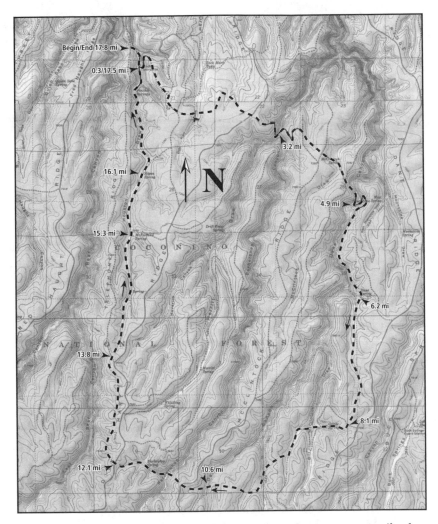

The trail turns southeast and descends into Dane Canyon at **4.9** miles but climbs only partway up the east side of the canyon before turning south. The U-Bar Trail stays along the east side of Dane Canyon to the ruins of an old cabin at Dane Spring, **6.2** miles. South of the spring the U-Bar Trail heads south up an unnamed drainage. Notice how the forest mix changes from nearly pure ponderosa pine on the sunny ridges to a mix of ponderosa pine, Douglas fir, and white fir in the shady draws. At the head of the draw, the trail emerges onto a flat, crosses a road, and meets the Barbershop Trail at **8.1** miles.

Turn right on the Barbershop Trail to continue the loop and follow the trail west into a shallow draw containing seasonal Coyote Spring. The Barbershop Trail continues west and crosses Bill McClintock Draw before turning south along a road through a meadow. Watch carefully for the point where the trail leaves the road to climb southwest over another ridge. The trail crosses a second ridge before dropping into Dane Canyon at 10.6 miles. Continue west on the Barbershop Trail past Barbershop Spring and across a maintained forest road to meet the Houston Brothers Trail at 12.1 miles.

Turn right on the Houston Brothers Trail and head north. The trail parallels the road until crossing it at 13.8 miles. Continue north along the trail as it descends into the head of Houston Draw. As the draw grows deeper, the trail passes through delightful aspen groves and alpine meadows. At mile 15.3 you'll pass McFarland Spring, and at 16.1 miles, Aspen Spring. Finally, at 17.5 miles you'll reach the trail junction at Pinchot Cabin, completing the loop. Turn left and hike 0.3 mile up the old road to FR 139A and your vehicle.

Pinchot Cabin was named for Gifford Pinchot, the first chief of the U.S. Forest Service. Once used as a fireguard station, the cabin has been restored but is no longer used. The other two historic cabins are Buck Springs Cabin (see "Going Farther") and General Springs Cabin, which is on hike #38.

GOING FARTHER

An obvious side hike starts from the trail junction at 8.1 miles. Turn left and hike 0.7 mile east, crossing Yeager Canyon and a forest road, to reach historic Buck Springs Cabin.

Another side hike takes you to a spectacular viewpoint on the edge of the Mogollon Rim. From the trail junction at 12.1 miles, turn left on the Houston Brothers Trail and hike 2.1 miles, crossing Forest Road 300 and the historic General Crook Trail just before reaching the rim.

38. Tunnel Trail

RATING	🚶 🚶 🚶
DISTANCE	1.0 mile round-trip
HIKING TIME	1 hour
ELEVATION GAIN	370 feet
HIGH POINT	7,279 feet
EFFORT	Easy Walk
BEST SEASON	Summer, fall
WATER	Tunnel Spring
PERMITS/CONTACT	None/Coconino National Forest, (928) 527-3600, www.fs.usda.gov/coconino
MAPS	USGS Dane Canyon, Kehl Ridge
NOTES	Leashed dogs welcome

THE HIKE

This short hike into the headwaters of the East Verde River follows a short section of the Arizona Trail on the edge of the Mogollon Rim.

GETTING THERE

From Strawberry on AZ 87 north of Payson, drive 9.8 miles north and turn right onto Forest Road 300 (Rim Road). Continue 12.5 miles and park at the General Springs trailhead on the left side of the road. The access roads are dirt and may be impassable during winter or wet weather. Elevation 7,277 feet, GPS coordinates N34°27.236'; W111°15.026'

THE TRAIL

Cross the Rim Road (FR 300) and follow Colonel Devin Trail (also used by the Arizona Trail) south down a drainage. After 0.3 mile turn left on the Tunnel Trail and follow the trail 0.2 mile up a side ravine to the northeast. The trail ends at the mouth of an old railroad tunnel.

The Colonel Devin Trail was named after Colonel Thomas C. Devin, who led a U.S. Army detachment from Fort Whipple in Prescott in search of some Apaches. The tunnel is about all that is left of an ambitious plan to build a railroad from the mines in Globe to connect with the main-line railroad in Flagstaff. The railroad company, Arizona Mineral Belt

General Springs Cabin, at the Tunnel Trail trailhead, is one of three restored historic cabins on the Cabin Loop Trail System.

Railroad, never had enough money to complete the project and finally abandoned it.

At the trailhead, a sign commemorates the Battle of Big Dry Wash, where the U.S. Army engaged members of the White Mountain Apache tribe on July 17, 1882. A band of about 60 Apache warriors left their reservation and headed west. Along the way some members of the band ambushed and killed four policemen from San Carlos. The band headed northwest toward the Mogollon Rim and local settlers demanded protection from the U.S. Army. The leader of the band, Na-tio-tish, intended to reach General Springs, but noticed that they were being trailed by a single cavalry troop and decided to lay an ambush about 7.0 miles north of General Springs.

The cavalry company's chief scout discovered the ambush and warned the troop's leader, Captain Adna R. Chaffee. During the night, reinforcements came in the form of four more companies from Fort Apache. For some reason Na-tio-tish did not post lookouts and the army was able to attack the Apaches from across the rim of the canyon and also from both flanks. The battle lasted from 3 p.m. until nightfall, when a heavy thunderstorm struck. Under cover of the storm and darkness, the surviving Apaches slipped away on foot. This was the last major battle between

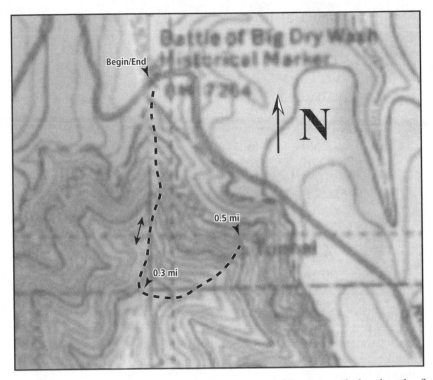

Native Americans and the U.S. Army, though Geronimo led a band of renegade Chiricahua Apache until his capture in 1886. Apache attacks continued in Arizona until 1900.

The trailhead is also the site of historic General Springs Cabin, once used as a fireguard station.

GOING FARTHER

From the junction of the Tunnel and Colonel Devin Trails, you can hike south on the Colonel Devin Trail down into the headwaters of the East Verde River. Another, easier option is to hike north from the trailhead, following the easy Fred Haught Trail along General Springs Canyon. This latter trail is part of the Cabin Loop trail system, and you can connect with other trails in the loop for a multiday backpack trip (see hike #37 in this guide).

39. Horton Creek

RATING	🚶 🚶 🚶 🚶
DISTANCE	6.4 miles round-trip
HIKING TIME	5 hours
ELEVATION GAIN	1,215 feet
HIGH POINT	6,680 feet
EFFORT	Moderate Workout
BEST SEASON	Summer, fall
WATER	Horton Creek
PERMITS/CONTACT	None/Tonto National Forest, (602) 225-5200, www.fs.usda.gov/tonto
MAPS	USGS Promontory Butte
NOTES	Leashed dogs welcome. You may encounter horses and mountain bikes.

THE HIKE

This scenic and cool hike in the ponderosa pine forest follows perennial Horton Creek to its source at a spring high under the ramparts of the Mogollon Rim.

The Horton Creek Trail closely follows Horton Creek, which tumbles down from a spring high under the Mogollon Rim.

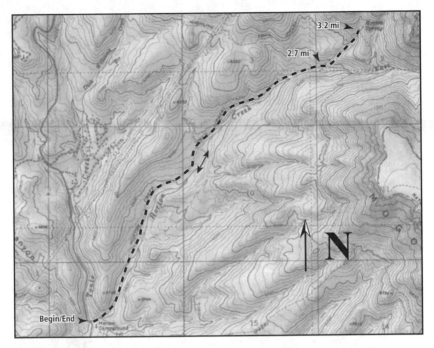

GETTING THERE

From Payson, drive 16.2 miles east on AZ 260 and turn left on Forest Highway 289. Drive 0.9 mile to Horton Creek Campground and park at the trailhead. Elevation 5,466 feet, GPS coordinates N34°20.382'; W111°05.736'

THE TRAIL

The Horton Creek Trail stays on the northwest side of Horton Creek as it follows the creek upstream to the northeast. Walking is easy on this popular trail and the creek is never too far away. Several meadows offer views of the rim country. When the trail begins to steepen, just below the Mogollon Rim at **2.7** miles, you'll cross the Highline Trail. Continue on the Horton Creek Trail to its end at Horton Springs.

GOING FARTHER

It's possible to do a 6.5-mile loop by turning right on the Highline Trail at 2.7 miles and hiking south to the Merrick Trail at mile 4.3. Near the lower end of the Merrick Trail at 5.9 miles, a spur trail turns right and returns to Horton Creek Campground. The trailhead is across the road.

The southern Mazatzal Mountains are typical of the rugged mountain ranges in central Arizona.

CENTRAL HIGHLANDS

South of the Mogollon Rim, the character of Arizona abruptly changes from high plateaus to rugged mountains and deep valleys. Part of the basin and range country that encompasses all of central, southern, and western Arizona, the Central Highlands feature several mountain ranges that have extensive trail networks and some of the best hiking in the state.

The highest ranges reach just under 8,000 feet in elevation and are crowned by stands of pine and fir forest, while the lower ranges are primarily desert. Some of the mountains have gentle, plateau-like summits, while others have rocky peaks. A common feature of all these ranges is deep, rugged canyons.

The hikes in this section range from trails through mountain forest, to rocky summits with great views, and desert canyons that feature seasonal streams and spring wildflower shows. The Mazatzal and Superstition Mountains in particular have many miles of trails to enjoy. Summers are hot and the higher elevations are snow-covered in the winter, so spring and fall are the best hiking seasons in these mountains. But the lowest elevations, such as the western Superstition Mountains, are mild and pleasant during the winter.

CENTRAL HIGHLANDS

40. Woodchute Trail

RATING	🚶 🚶 🚶
DISTANCE	8.8 miles round-trip
HIKING TIME	5 hours
ELEVATION GAIN	710 feet
HIGH POINT	7,709 feet
EFFORT	Moderate Workout
BEST SEASON	Summer, fall
WATER	None
PERMITS/CONTACT	None/Prescott National Forest, (928) 443-8000, www.fs.usda.gov/prescott
MAPS	USGS Hickey Mountain, Munds Draw
NOTES	Leashed dogs welcome

THE HIKE

Though a longer hike, this trail is relatively easy due to the moderate elevation change. There are several places along the trail with views of the Verde Valley, and the end of the hike features a panoramic view of the western Mogollon Rim.

GETTING THERE

From Jerome, drive about 7 miles west on AZ 89A to the pass at the top of Mingus Mountain. Turn right on the Potato Patch Campground road and drive 0.4 mile to the Woodchute trailhead on the left. Elevation 7,063 feet, GPS coordinates N34°42.441'; W112°09.118'

THE TRAIL

The Woodchute Trail heads through a low saddle and then follows a road a short distance to Powerline Tank. At 0.8 mile the road turns west; turn left onto the foot trail and follow it around the east sides of a couple of hills. The brushy hillside opens up for some good views of the Verde Valley to the east. After passing around the east side of a third hill, the Woodchute Trail drops into a ravine and then climbs north onto Woodchute Mountain, reaching the rim of this gently sloping mesa at mile 3.3.

A huge alligator juniper, named for the alligator-like texture of its bark, along the Woodchute Trail.

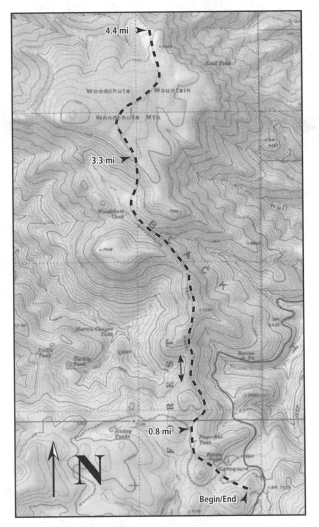

Follow the trail across Woodchute Mountain to its north rim. Although the trail continues down the north slopes of the mountain, the rim is a good turnaround point. Before you start back, be sure to take in the views of the Mogollon Rim to the north across the Verde River Canyon.

41. Granite Mountain Trail

RATING	🚶 🚶 🚶 🚶
DISTANCE	7.2 miles round-trip
HIKING TIME	5 hours
ELEVATION GAIN	1,540 feet
HIGH POINT	7,110 feet
EFFORT	Moderate Workout
BEST SEASON	Spring–fall
WATER	None
PERMITS/CONTACT	None/Prescott National Forest, (928) 443-8000, www.fs.usda.gov/prescott
MAPS	USGS Iron Springs, Jerome Canyon; USFS Granite Mountain Wilderness
NOTES	Leashed dogs welcome

THE HIKE

A very enjoyable hike through a rugged landscape of granite boulders, chaparral brush, pinyon-juniper woodland, and tall ponderosa pines, ending at a viewpoint overlooking the Sierra Prieta ("pretty mountains" in Spanish).

GETTING THERE

From downtown Prescott, drive 4.5 miles northwest on Montezuma Street, which first becomes Whipple Street, then Irons Springs Road, and turn right on Granite Basin Road. Continue 3.6 miles to the Metate trailhead. Elevation 5,687 feet, GPS coordinates N34°36.831'; W112°32.990'

THE TRAIL

Follow the Granite Mountain Trail across a dry wash and stay right at the junction with the Little Granite Mountain Trail. The Granite Mountain Trail heads generally northeast, climbing gradually up a valley studded with granite boulders. As you proceed, you'll start to get glimpses of Granite Mountain Wall, a world-class rock climbing area, high above to the right.

At **1.8** miles, the trail reaches Blair Pass; stay right to remain on the Granite Mountain Trail. Now the trail heads generally north and climbs

Granite Mountain, a world-class rock climbing area, towers above the Granite Mountain Trail.

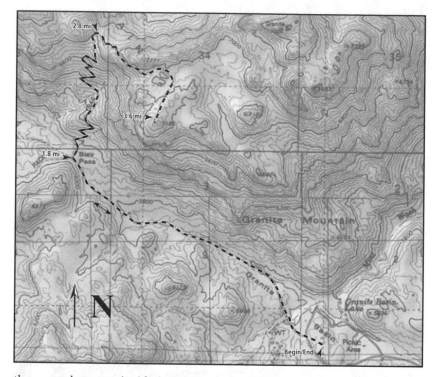

the rugged mountainside in a series of switchbacks. After the trail climbs into a saddle at **2.8** miles, it turns southeast and works its way onto the broad summit area of Granite Mountain. After wandering through a park-like area of ponderosa pines and granite slabs, the trail heads south to end at a viewpoint above Granite Mountain Wall, at **3.6** miles.

GOING FARTHER

The viewpoint, labeled as 7,186 feet on the topo map, is not the summit of Granite Mountain. If you want to bag the actual highpoint, leave the trail in the park-like valley about 0.3 mile before the end of the trail and head cross-country northeast up the valley. You'll get glimpses of the summit, marked "7626" on the topo map, up ahead—just keep walking toward it. At the end of the valley, under the summit, work your way to the top via the south slopes of the peak.

A loop hike can be done by turning left on the Little Granite Mountain Trail near the trailhead and following it around Little Granite Mountain and back to Blair Pass. From here, you can return to the trailhead on the Granite Mountain Trail.

42. Pine Mountain

RATING	🚶 🚶 🚶 🚶
DISTANCE	13.0-mile loop
HIKING TIME	8 hours or 2 days
ELEVATION GAIN	1,640 feet
HIGH POINT	6,714 feet
EFFORT	Prepare to Perspire
BEST SEASON	Spring–fall
WATER	Nelson Place Spring, Beehouse Spring, Bishop Spring, Pine Spring, and Willow Spring
PERMITS/CONTACT	None/Prescott National Forest, (928) 443-8000, www.fs.usda.gov/prescott
MAPS	USGS Tule Mesa
NOTES	Leashed dogs welcome

THE HIKE

This enjoyable loop takes you over the summit of Pine Mountain, at 6,714 feet the highest point in the Pine Mountain Wilderness.

GETTING THERE

From Cordes Junction on Interstate 17, drive north 6.1 miles to the Dugas Interchange and turn right on County Road 171, which becomes Forest Road 68. Continue 10.9 miles and turn right on FR 68 (FR 68G continues straight ahead). Drive 6.6 miles to Pine Mountain trailhead at the end of the road. The access roads are dirt and may be impassable during winter or wet weather. Elevation 5,096 feet, GPS coordinates N34°19.576'; W111°50.189'

THE TRAIL

From the trailhead, follow the Pine Mountain Trail southeast up Sycamore Creek. This first section of trail passes Nelson Place, an old homestead where the remains of the fruit orchard are still visible, and Nelson Place Spring. At **0.8** mile, turn right on the Beehouse Spring Trail to start the loop.

The trail climbs up a canyon to the southwest, passing Beehouse Spring, and meets the Pine Flat Trail at the head of the canyon at **1.9** miles.

Hiking the Pine Mountain Trail just below the summit.

Stay left on the Pine Flat Trail and follow it south through a broad saddle and then down into the head of South Prong Sycamore Creek. The trail stays near the bed of the drainage for a while then climbs out on the east side to another trail junction in a saddle at **3.8** miles. Turn sharply left here and follow the Verde Rim Trail northeast past Bishop Spring. At **5.3** miles stay right at the junction with the Bishop Creek Trail and continue on the Verde Rim Trail as it contours around the heads of several tributary canyons, heading generally southeast. The trail finally reaches its namesake, the Verde Rim, and follows the rim northeast. At **8.1** miles another trail comes in from the left; bear right on the Verde Rim Trail and follow it to the high point of the loop at **8.7** miles. The trail doesn't quite go over the summit of Pine Mountain here, but you can climb a few yards east to reach it. The 360-degree view includes the wild canyons of

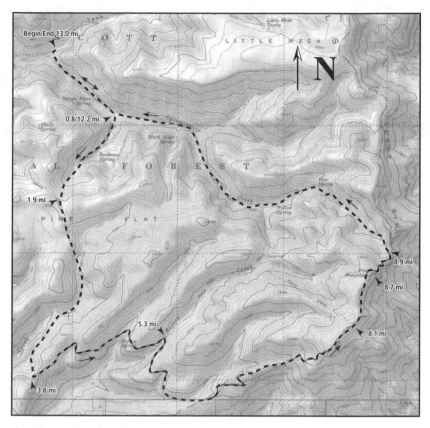

the Verde River to the east as well as the northwest slopes of the rugged Mazatzal Mountains.

After reaching the summit, follow the Verde Rim Trail north to a saddle at **8.9** miles and turn left on the Pine Mountain Trail. This trail drops down the head of Sycamore Creek, passing Pine Spring and Willow Spring, and meeting the Beehouse Spring Trail at **12.2** miles. This closes the loop; stay right to return to the trailhead.

43. Y Bar Basin–Barnhardt Canyon Loop

RATING	🚶 🚶 🚶 🚶 🚶
DISTANCE	13.5-mile loop
HIKING TIME	8 hours or 2 days
ELEVATION GAIN	2,400 feet
HIGH POINT	6,580 feet
EFFORT	Prepare to Perspire
BEST SEASON	Spring–fall
WATER	Seasonal at Y Bar Tanks, Chilson Spring
PERMITS/CONTACT	None/Tonto National Forest, (602) 225-5200, www.fs.usda.gov/tonto
MAPS	USGS Mazatzal Peak; USFS Mazatzal Wilderness
NOTES	Leashed dogs welcome. Much of the Mazatzal Mountains were burned in the Willow wildfire in 2004, so expect occasional deadfall on the trails.

THE HIKE

The classic loop around Mazatzal Peak, this hike uses a portion of the Mazatzal Divide Trail to connect two east-side trails.

GETTING THERE

From Payson, drive 13.1 miles south on AZ 87 and turn right on Barnhardt Road. Drive 5.2 miles to Barnhardt trailhead at the end of the road. The access road is dirt and may be impassable during winter or wet weather. Elevation 4,175 feet, GPS coordinates N34°05.561'; W111°25.279'

THE TRAIL

Leave the trailhead on the Y Bar Basin Trail (shown as the Shake Tree Trail on the topo). At first, the trail switchbacks southwest up a rocky slope through pinyon-juniper woodland, but then starts climbing steadily along the east slopes below Suicide Ridge. The trail climbs along the slopes above Shake Tree Canyon, then crosses a drainage where you may find water in the spring. At **4.0** miles, the trail crosses the saddle between Cactus Ridge and Mazatzal Peak, then descends steeply into Y Bar Basin. You may find water at **4.6** miles where the trail crosses the drainage

Hiking the Barnhardt Trail through rugged Barnhardt Canyon.

above Y Bar Tanks. If not, you can follow the drainage a couple hundred yards downstream to the tanks themselves, which nearly always have water. Now, the trail turns northwest and starts climbing up a drainage. At **5.7** miles, turn right onto the Mazatzal Divide Trail in the saddle southwest of Mazatzal Peak. Windsor Spring, shown on the topo map, has water only after a wet winter.

Follow the Mazatzal Divide Trail north as it contours below the impressive west face of Mazatzal Peak. This section provides excellent views of the remote wilderness west of the Mazatzal Crest. At **8.5** miles, the trail contours into Barnhardt Saddle at the head of Barnhardt Canyon.

Those who plan to camp should turn left and stay on the Mazatzal Divide Trail less than 1.0 mile to Chilson Camp, which is the best campsite on the loop. A former cowboy line camp in a pinyon-juniper flat, Chilson Spring provides water except in very dry years.

To continue the loop, turn right on the Barnhardt Trail and follow it generally east. The well-graded trail descends gradually around the head drainages of Barnhardt Canyon. At **10.2** miles, the Casterson Seep Trail comes in from the left; stay right on the Barnhardt Trail and continue descending to the east. After the trail rounds the north end of a brushy ridge, it crosses a drainage where there is a seasonal waterfall.

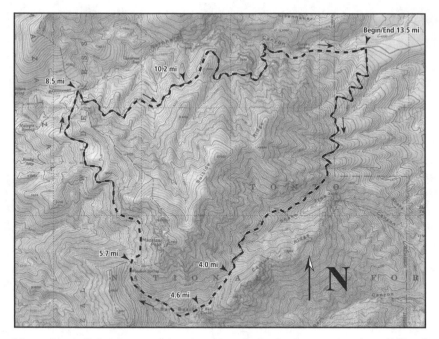

Now the trail begins working its way through the spectacular cliffs of lower Barnhardt Canyon, and finally descends to the north in a series of short switchbacks. After the trail levels out just above the canyon bottom, it again heads east, accompanied by the musical sound of water in the creek below—always a treat in the desert. After about a mile of this pleasant walking, the trail emerges from the canyon and arrives at the trailhead.

GOING FARTHER

The northern Mazatzal Mountains, part of the Mazatzal Wilderness, provide many days of hiking on a large network of trails. Most of these trails are long and remote, not to mention little used and faint, so extended exploration of the area requires multiday backpack trips, carefully planned around water sources.

There are a couple of side hikes worth taking from the Y Bar–Barnhardt Loop, which are most practical if you're making it a two-day trip. From the saddle at Windsor Spring, you can turn left and hike the Mazatzal Divide Trail 1.5 miles south to the saddle between Bear Spring and Fisher Spring. The forest in this area, above Y Bar Basin, was especially hard hit by the Willow Fire. The north slope forest of ponderosa pine and Douglas fir was almost completely destroyed in the crown fire that swept through the basin.

Another, longer side hike leaves Barnhardt Saddle and continues north on the Mazatzal Divide Trail past the turnoff to Chilson Camp to the turnoff to Horse Camp Seep. Turn left and walk down to the seep, a small spring set below open slabs of Mazatzal quartzite and just above a small dry waterfall. There are campsites here, 3.1 miles from Barnhardt Saddle, and for a real treat, work your way around the left side of the dry fall about 0.3 mile downstream to the top of the high cliffs bounding the canyon of the North Fork of Deadman Creek.

44. Browns Peak

RATING	🚶 🚶 🚶 🚶
DISTANCE	4.0 miles round-trip
HIKING TIME	3 to 4 hours
ELEVATION GAIN	1,960 feet
HIGH POINT	7,657 feet
EFFORT	Prepare to Perspire
BEST SEASON	Spring–fall
WATER	None
PERMITS/CONTACT	None/Tonto National Forest, (602) 225-5200, www.fs.usda.gov/tonto
MAPS	USGS Four Peaks
NOTES	Leashed dogs welcome

THE HIKE

This hike leads to the top of Browns Peak, at 7,657 feet the highest of the Four Peaks. Four Peaks is visible on the eastern skyline from much of the greater Phoenix area and on clear winter days treats the desert dwellers to a vision of snowcapped mountains. As the highest peak in the southern Mazatzal Mountains, the summit offers stunning views.

GETTING THERE

From Mesa, at the junction of AZ 202 and AZ 87, drive 27.6 miles on AZ 87 north and turn right on the Four Peaks Road. Continue 10.7 miles and bear right. After 5.6 miles, turn sharply right at a saddle on the crest of the Mazatzal Mountains. Drive 1.3 miles south to Lone Pine trailhead at the end of the road. The access roads are dirt and may be impassable during winter or wet weather. Elevation 5,708 feet, GPS coordinates N33°42.341'; W111°20.280'

THE TRAIL

Leave the trailhead on the Browns Peak Trail and follow it up a couple of switchbacks on the slope just south of the trailhead. After the trail gains the main crest of the Mazatzal Mountains, it climbs steadily up this ridge to the south. It then contours around the east side of the ridge, where it

Browns Peak is the left-hand and highest of the Four Peaks in the southern Mazatzal Mountains.

meets the Amethyst Trail coming in from the left. Stay right and continue to the saddle below Browns Peak at **1.6** miles.

From here a cross-country climb of less than 0.4 mile takes you to the summit of Browns Peak. You can go about this several different ways, but probably the easiest is to climb directly toward the peak until you reach the first cliffs, then work your way right along the base of the cliffs to a major west-facing ravine at **1.8** miles. Hike up this ravine to its end. You'll encounter a couple of places where you'll need to use your hands. From the top of the ravine, scramble a short distance east to the summit.

GOING FARTHER
An alternative to the Browns Peak Trail, the Four Peaks Trail also leaves Lone Pine trailhead and heads around the east slopes below the main

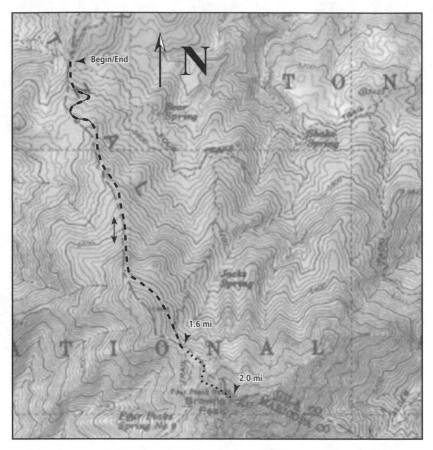

ridge crest. At 1 mile, turn right on the Amethyst Trail and follow it uphill to the junction with the Browns Peak Trail at 1.8 miles. Now turn left and hike 0.1 mile to the saddle below Browns Peak. This route is 0.3 mile longer than the Browns Peak Trail.

45. Barks Canyon

RATING	🚶 🚶 🚶 🚶
DISTANCE	4.9-mile loop
HIKING TIME	4 hours
ELEVATION GAIN	1,370 feet
HIGH POINT	3,800 feet
EFFORT	Moderate Workout
BEST SEASON	Fall–spring
WATER	Seasonal in Barks Canyon
PERMITS/CONTACT	None/Tonto National Forest, (602) 225-5200, www.fs.usda.gov/tonto
MAPS	USGS Weavers Needle; USFS Superstition Wilderness
NOTES	Leashed dogs welcome

THE HIKE

This enjoyable loop combines popular, well-defined trails with a short bit of easy cross-country hiking to create a remarkable wilderness feel for this hike through the rugged Superstition Mountains—affectionately known as the "Sups" by several generations of enthusiastic hikers.

GETTING THERE

From Apache Junction, drive about 5 miles east on U.S. 60 and turn left on Peralta Road. Continue 7.2 miles to Peralta trailhead at the end of the road. The access roads are dirt and may be impassable during winter or wet weather. Elevation 2,414 feet, GPS coordinates N33°23.843'; W111°20.871'

THE TRAIL

Start the loop on the well-traveled Peralta Trail, which climbs northeast up scenic Peralta Canyon, named for a Mexican who supposedly had a rich gold mine in the Superstition Mountains and was massacred by American Indians. The Peralta saga began the persistent myth of a rich gold mine in the Superstitions. This myth was perpetuated by the story of the Lost Dutchman Mine, where a German prospector, Jacob Waltz, on his deathbed in Phoenix, supposedly said that his gold mine was located where the tip of the shadow of Weavers Needle fell at 4 p.m.

Hiking through the Sonoran Desert in the Superstition Mountains—known locally as the "Sups."

When the trail reaches the head of Peralta Canyon at Fremont Saddle at 1.9 miles, you'll have a fine view of the spire of Weavers Needle, one of the most distinctive landmarks of the Superstition Mountains. Just a quick glance at the incredibly complex and rugged country surrounding Weavers Needle shows how difficult it would be to locate a lost mine. Furthermore, Waltz didn't specify the day of the year! Over the course of a year, the tip of the shadow of Weavers Needle at 4 p.m. traces many square miles of wilderness. And to add insult to injury, geologists insist that the volcanic western Superstition Mountains contain no gold-bearing formations. Nevertheless, several generations of prospectors searched for the mine, filed claims, left the wreckage of abandoned camps and mines, and squabbled over mining rights. In some cases there were mysterious deaths associated with the mountains. Up through the mid-1960s, hikers were likely to encounter very unfriendly prospectors. The U.S. Forest Service finally put an end to all this silliness by withdrawing the entire Weavers Needle area from any further mineral location or mining.

The real wealth of the "Sups" lies in its rugged, remote beauty, only a few miles from the edge of a city of five million people. To experience a bit of this remoteness, head northeast from Fremont Saddle on an informal

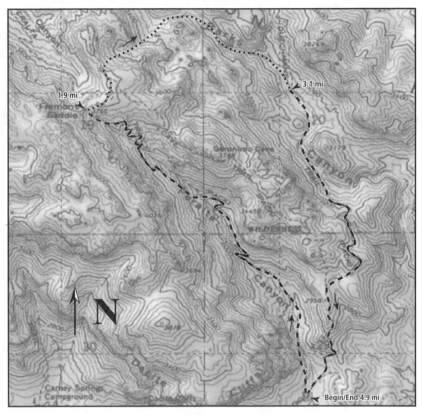

trail. Follow the trail to its end at a viewpoint at the north end of the flat mesa, then head east and work your way cross-country down into Barks Canyon. There are several ways you can descend the short cliffs bounding the mesa, but all routes end up in Barks Canyon as long as you head downhill to the northeast. Turn right and hike downstream along the bed of Barks Canyon. At 3.1 miles, the heavily traveled Bluff Spring Trail descends into the canyon from the left. There are often seasonal pools in this section of Barks Canyon.

Turn right and follow the Bluff Spring Trail down Barks Canyon, over a ridge, and back to Peralta trailhead.

GOING FARTHER
An extensive network of trails covers the entire Superstition Mountains and provides many days of enjoyable day hiking and backpack trips of up to four or five days. (For examples, see hikes #46 and #47 in this guide.)

46. Dutchmans Loop

RATING	🚶 🚶 🚶 🚶
DISTANCE	17.4-mile loop
HIKING TIME	9 hours or 2 days
ELEVATION GAIN	1,060 feet
HIGH POINT	3,380 feet
EFFORT	Prepare to Perspire
BEST SEASON	Fall–spring
WATER	Seasonal at Crystal Spring, Holmes Spring, La Barge Spring, Music Canyon Spring, Charlebois Spring, White Rock Spring, and Peralta Spring
PERMITS/CONTACT	None/Tonto National Forest, (602) 225-5200, www.fs.usda.gov/tonto
MAPS	USGS Weavers Needle, Goldfield; USFS Superstition Wilderness
NOTES	Leashed dogs welcome. Some of the trails, and especially the north end of the Peralta Trail, are not shown accurately on the topo maps. Other trails are incorrectly named on the topos. Refer to the USFS Superstition Wilderness map for current trail information.

THE HIKE

The classic loop through the western Superstition Mountains, this hike circles Weavers Needle and takes you deep into the rugged canyons of the "Sups" all on well-traveled and well-graded trails. Although you can do this as a very long day hike, it is much more enjoyable as an overnight hike.

GETTING THERE

From Apache Junction, drive about 5 miles east on U.S. 60 and turn left on Peralta Road. Continue 7.2 miles to Peralta trailhead at the end of the road. The access roads are dirt and may be impassable during winter or wet weather. Elevation 2,414 feet, GPS coordinates N33°23.843'; W111°20.871'

The pinnacles of Miners Needle seen from the Dutchmans Trail near Miners Summit.

THE TRAIL

From Peralta trailhead, head east on the Dutchmans Trail. The trail climbs over a low desert ridge studded with giant saguaro cactus, then heads east along the base of the hills. Speaking of cactus, stay away from the cuddly-looking yellow cactus, appropriately named teddy-bear cholla. Also known as "jumping cholla," this cactus has spines that are razor-sharp and microscopically barbed. Even a light brush against the cactus results in burrs sticking to your skin or clothing and breaking off from the plant. In fact, that's how this cactus propagates, by hitching rides on unlucky animals. The best way to remove a cholla burr is to have someone else lift it off with two sticks. Any remaining spines will have to be removed with tweezers.

At **2.6** miles, the Coffee Flat Trail comes in from the right; stay left on the Dutchmans Trail and follow it as it makes a sharp turn to the

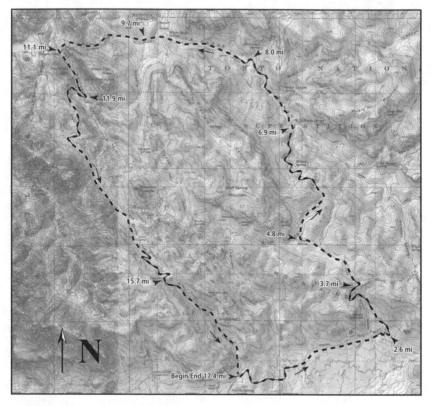

northwest and starts climbing up the small canyon east of Miners Needle. At the saddle at Miners Summit, **3.7** miles, stay left on the Dutchmans Trail as the Whiskey Spring Trail forks right. The Dutchmans Trail now descends to the northwest, crosses a low saddle, and meets the Bluff Spring Trail at Crystal Spring, at mile **4.8**. Turn right and continue on the Dutchmans Trail as it drops north down Bluff Spring Canyon. Soon the trail climbs out onto the slopes on the west side of the canyon and stays there as it works its way generally north. After passing the short side trail to Holmes Spring, the Dutchmans Trail descends into La Barge Canyon at **6.9** miles. Here, the Red Tanks Trail comes in from the left and La Barge Spring is located just a few yards up this trail. There is plenty of camping on the flats along the canyon bottom.

Turn left and follow the Dutchmans Trail down La Barge Canyon. The trail soon passes the short spur trail to Music Canyon Spring, and at **8.0** miles arrives at Charlebois Spring and the Peters Trail Junction. Avoid camping at this badly overused site and continue left, down La Barge

Canyon. There are some nice campsites in the vicinity of White Rock Spring, where the trail leaves La Barge Canyon at Marsh Valley.

At **9.7** miles, the Needle Canyon Trail comes in from the left; continue straight ahead on the Dutchmans Trail. The trail now climbs east over Bull Pass at the north end of Black Top Mesa, then descends into East Boulder Canyon at **11.1** miles.

Turn left on the Peralta Canyon Trail and follow it south along East Boulder Canyon. At **11.9** miles the trail emerges into a pleasant little flat and the Needle Cutoff Trail comes in from the left. There are often seasonal pools in the canyon bed and there are plenty of campsites in this area.

Stay on the Peralta Trail and follow it west as it switchbacks over a ridge, then heads south. The trail works its way up the slopes on the west side of East Boulder Canyon for over 1.0 mile before descending to the remains of an old miners camp at Peralta Spring. The trail continues south-southeast along the very scenic upper reaches of Peralta Canyon, passing Pinyon Camp with its small stand of pinyon pines—a rare sight in the western Superstitions. Seasonal pools can sometimes be found in the canyon bed just east of the camp. The Peralta Trail heads on up East Boulder Canyon, finally climbing via a broad switchback to Fremont Saddle at **15.7** miles. Follow the Peralta Trail southwest down Peralta Canyon to the Peralta trailhead.

GOING FARTHER

There are many possible side hikes and alternative trails along this loop. At Miners Summit, you could turn right on the Whiskey Spring Trail and use it and the Red Tanks Trail to rejoin the main loop at La Barge Spring. Just west of Marsh Valley, you could turn left on the Needle Canyon Trail and follow this trail over Terrapin Pass, past the impressive east face of Weavers Needle, and over Bluff Saddle to join the Bluff Spring Trail. Turn left to return to Peralta trailhead.

For a nice view of the Weavers Needle country from an unusual vantage point, leave the Dutchmans Trail at Bull Pass and hike south on an informal trail that leads to the top of Black Top Mesa. After you've enjoyed the view, look around for hieroglyphics pecked into the rock, which have a few words in Spanish.

47. Fireline Loop

RATING	🚶 🚶 🚶 🚶
DISTANCE	15.0-mile loop
HIKING TIME	10 hours or 2 days
ELEVATION GAIN	2,190 feet
HIGH POINT	5,470 feet
EFFORT	Prepare to Perspire
BEST SEASON	Spring, fall
WATER	Campaign Creek, Whiskey Spring, Brushy Spring, and seasonal in lower Pine Creek, at the Reevis Ranch site, and upper Campaign Creek
PERMITS/CONTACT	None/Tonto National Forest, (602) 225-5200, www.fs.usda.gov/tonto
MAPS	USGS Two Bar Mountain, Haunted Canyon, Iron Mountain, Pinyon Mountain; USFS Superstition Wilderness
NOTES	Leashed dogs welcome. Some of the trails, including the Reevis Gap and Two Bar Ridge Trails, are not shown on the topo maps.

THE HIKE

This fine loop encompasses a large portion of the remote eastern Superstition Mountains, passing through ponderosa pine forest and the remains of a historic ranch.

GETTING THERE

From Globe, at the junction of U.S. 60 and AZ 188, drive 22 miles west on AZ 88 and turn left on Campaign Creek Road. Drive 23 miles to the Campaign trailhead at a gate. (The road continues to Reevis Mountain School, which is private property.) The access roads are dirt, follow washes that are prone to flooding, and may be impassable during winter or wet weather. Elevation 3,251 feet, GPS coordinates N33°31.810'; W111°04.846'

Ponderosa pines shade part of the Reevis Ranch Trail along the Fireline Loop.

THE TRAIL

Walk past the Reevis Mountain School on the Campaign Trail and continue up Campaign Creek, which has a perennial stream along this section. At **0.7** mile, turn right on the Reevis Gap Trail (not shown on the topo map), which promptly climbs over a low ridge, crosses a dry wash, then climbs steadily west to a saddle unmarked on the topo map but known as Reevis Gap. Just west of this saddle, at **3.0** miles, the Two Bar Ridge Trail comes in from the right (not shown on the topo map). Stay left on the Reevis Gap Trail and continue down to cross Pine Creek, where there is seasonal water and some fine campsites among the pinyon pines.

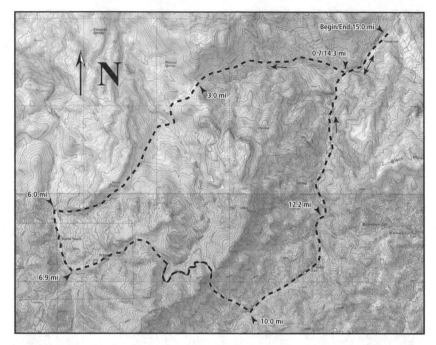

From Pine Creek, the Reevis Gap Trail climbs gradually southwest over a small saddle and then descends to meet the Reevis Ranch Trail at **6.0** miles. Turn left on the Reevis Ranch Trail and follow it south past the old apple orchard to the ruins of Reevis Ranch. There is seasonal water in Reevis Creek and plenty of campsites in the area.

Reevis Ranch was a working ranch accessed by a long winding road from the north. After the family sold the ranch to the U.S. Forest Service, the area was added to the wilderness and the old road became the Reevis Ranch Trail. For a time, the old ranch house was preserved as a historic site and emergency shelter, but then some campers burned the house to the ground. Volunteers cleaned up the mess and today only the foundation remains.

Continue south on the Reevis Ranch Trail to the **6.9**-mile point and turn left on the Fireline Trail. This trail climbs past Whiskey Spring and heads generally east over a saddle, then down into upper Pine Creek. There is usually no water and certainly no camping in this steep canyon headwaters. After leaving Pine Creek, the trail contours for a bit and then climbs gradually to a saddle northeast of Mound Mountain. A steep descent down a brushy ridge leads past Black Jack Spring (not shown on the topo map, but shown on the USFS wilderness map) to upper

Campaign Creek and some fine campsites under tall ponderosa pines at 10.0 miles. Many hikers familiar with the lower western Superstitions are surprised to learn that there are tall pines in the eastern portion of the range.

The Fireline Trail was originally constructed by firefighters working a fire in the 1950s. Back then, the wilderness was only administratively protected and the U.S. Forest Service felt it was necessary to use heavy equipment, including bulldozers, to fight the fire. Today, little evidence of the wildfire remains, but the bulldozer scars endure. This seems to justify the present Forest Service policy of not using mechanized tools to fight fires in wilderness areas. Although this has resulted in some very large and destructive fires—notably the Willow Fire that burned much of the Mazatzal Wilderness in 2006, the Kendrick Fire that burned all of Kendrick Mountain Wilderness, the fires that have burned all of the Pusch Ridge Wilderness in the Santa Catalina Mountains, and the large wildfires that periodically burn in the Blue Range Wilderness—it's best to look at these fires as nature's way of restoring balance to the forest ecosystem after a hundred years of mismanagement. The process of restoration is fascinating to watch, as wildflowers explode across the burned landscape during the summer rains, and brush and young trees take root.

Turn left and follow the Campaign Trail down Campaign Creek, which is usually dry except for seasonal Brushy Spring. The mix of pinyon pine, juniper, and chaparral brush covering the slopes is a distinct change from the vegetation in the more well-known western Superstitions. At 12.2 miles, you'll pass the turnoff to Mountain Spring; stay left on the Campaign Trail and continue on this long but gentle trail to the junction with Reevis Gap Trail at 14.3 miles, closing the loop. Stay right on the Campaign Trail and hike 0.7 mile to the Campaign trailhead.

GOING FARTHER

A recommended side hike takes you to the top of the highest point in the Superstition Mountains, 6,266-foot Mound Mountain. Leave the Fireline Trail on a cairned route that forks right just before the Fireline Trail descends into the bed of upper Pine Creek. This informal trail climbs south through pinyon-juniper woodland onto a ridge, passing a strange circular ruin. Continue up the ridge toward Mound Mountain, then work your way cross-country up the northwest slopes of the summit to avoid the worst of the brush. The view from this vantage point includes the classic skyline of the western Superstition crest, the reverse of the view seen from the Phoenix area. All around you lie the deep canyons of the Superstition Mountains.

Quaking aspen turn yellow, gold, and red during fall in Arizona's high country.

WHITE MOUNTAINS

Located at the eastern end of the Mogollon Rim in eastern Arizona, the White Mountains are Arizona's second highest mountain range. Essentially a high volcanic plateau with gently rounded summits, the White Mountains receive enough winter snow and late-summer rain to feature numerous mountain streams and alpine lakes. The mountains are the headwaters for several of the region's major rivers. The high plateaus are a beautiful mix of pine, fir, and aspen forest as well as alpine meadows.

In contrast to most of the hiking areas in the state, the White Mountains have less relief and it's possible to take long hikes with little elevation change. Elevations from 9,000 to 11,000 feet provide a complete escape from the summer heat. During the fall, extensive stands of quaking aspen paint the forest with bands of yellow and gold.

Trails in this section range from a route up to the high point of the White Mountains to trails in forested canyons. You can explore creeks, lakes, and waterfalls and can hike along the route of a historic railroad.

WHITE MOUNTAINS

48. Escudilla Mountain

RATING	🚶 🚶 🚶 🚶
DISTANCE	5.6 miles round-trip
HIKING TIME	4 hours
ELEVATION GAIN	1,220 feet
HIGH POINT	10,877 feet
EFFORT	Moderate Workout
BEST SEASON	Summer, fall
WATER	None
PERMITS/CONTACT	None/Apache-Sitgreaves National Forests, (928) 333-4301, www.fs.usda.gov/asnf
MAPS	USGS Escudilla Mountain
NOTES	Leashed dogs welcome. Most of the mountain burned during the catastrophic Wallow Fire of 2011, which was started by an abandoned campfire and burned 538,000 acres. It was the largest fire in Arizona history—the second-largest ever in America. Formerly heavily forested with aspen glades and alpine meadows, Escudilla Mountain was struck especially hard, where the fire crowned out and killed most of the trees. Smoke from the fire was detected in New York City and was visible from space.

THE HIKE

Escudilla Mountain is now an exercise in natural restoration; it will be interesting to watch how nature takes its course. At these elevations, the first tree to return is usually fast-growing quaking aspen, which regenerates directly from unburned roots and reaches heights of 10 or 20 feet in only a few years. So it's likely that the burned slopes will rapidly be covered by the slender white trunks and soft green leaves of the graceful trees. In the fall, the entire mountain will be slashed by yellow, orange, and red as the aspens change.

GETTING THERE

From Alpine at the junction of U.S. 180 and U.S. 191, drive 5.6 miles north on U.S. 180 and turn right on Terry Flat Road. Continue 3.9 miles,

Hiking through aspen meadows on the Escudilla Mountain Trail before the Wallow Fire of 2011.

then bear left at the junction with Terry Flat Loop Road. Drive 0.3 mile to Escudilla Mountain trailhead at Toolbox Draw, on the left. The access roads are dirt and may be impassable during winter or wet weather. Elevation 9,642 feet, GPS coordinates N33°55.201'; W109°07.035'

THE TRAIL
The hike follows the Escudilla Mountain Trail northeast and then north up steep slopes into Profanity Ridge and the mountain's summit plateau at **1.4** miles. The trail drops slightly through a saddle at **1.7** miles and

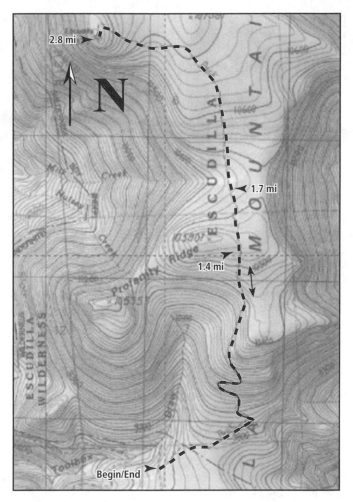

then makes the final ascent to the northwest and west, ending at Escudilla Lookout, a fire tower staffed during the fire season.

GOING FARTHER

The lookout, at 10,877 feet, is not the actual high point of the mountain. A cross-country hike of less than 1 mile leads north along the summit ridge to an unnamed peak that just breaks the 10,900-foot contour on the topo map. This hike may not be feasible at present due to deadfall from the burned forest.

49. Apache Railroad Trail

RATING	🚶 🚶 🚶 🚶
DISTANCE	19.8 miles one-way with shuttle
HIKING TIME	10 hours or 2 days
ELEVATION GAIN	420 feet
HIGH POINT	9,407 feet
EFFORT	Moderate Workout
BEST SEASON	Summer, fall
WATER	Big Lake, Burro Creek, West Fork Little Colorado River. The other lakes shown on the topo map are shallow and marshy and may be difficult to reach.
PERMITS/CONTACT	None/Apache-Sitgreaves National Forests, (928) 333-4301, www.fs.usda.gov/asnf
MAPS	USGS Big Lake North, Mount Baldy, Greer, Greens Peak
NOTES	Leashed dogs welcome. You may encounter mountain bikes and horses.

THE HIKE

This one-way hike follows the bed of the former Apache Railroad, originally built as a logging railroad and then operated as a scenic railroad. A portion of the rail bed has been opened as a recreational trail for non-motorized use. The trail climbs the gorgeous high plateau of the White Mountains, traversing vast alpine meadows and deep alpine spruce and fir forest. Aspen groves and numerous lakes add to the alpine feel. For those who wish to make an overnight trip, camping is just about unlimited anywhere along the trail.

GETTING THERE

To reach the endpoint of the hike from Springerville, drive approximately 17 miles west on AZ 260 and turn left into the Big Cienega trailhead. Elevation 9,166 feet, GPS coordinates N34°03.250'; W109°34.097'

To reach the starting point of the hike from the Big Cienega trailhead drive 1.6 miles west on AZ 260 and turn left on AZ 273. Continue 16.7 miles and bear right onto AZ 261. Continue 2.5 miles and turn right into Big Lake Recreation Area. Drive 2.9 miles, passing the campgrounds and boat ramps, and turn right on Forest Road 249E. Drive 1.6 miles, then

Big Lake near the start of the Apache Railroad Trail is a popular recreation area.

turn right and drive 0.2 mile to the Railroad Cove trailhead. The last 2 miles are dirt roads that may be impassable in wet weather. Access to Big Lake is closed during the winter. Elevation 8,996 feet, GPS coordinates N33°53.045'; W109°25.771'

THE TRAIL
From the Railroad Cove trailhead, follow the old railroad bed north. After skirting the northwest arm of Big Lake, the Apache Railroad Trail heads across an open alpine meadow toward Basin Lake, then turns northwest before reaching the lake. It crosses AZ 273 at 3.1 miles, then closely parallels the highway, following the northeast side of Burro Creek upstream and skirting the alpine spruce/fir forest. After passing through the broad saddle at the head of Burro Creek at 5.3 miles, the trail turns north, passes the road turnoff to the East Baldy trailhead and Gabaldon Campground,

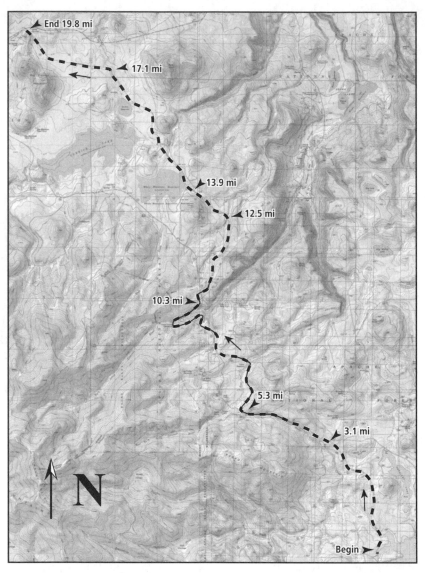

End 19.8 mi
17.1 mi
13.9 mi
12.5 mi
10.3 mi
5.3 mi
3.1 mi
N
Begin

and skirts the east edge of a meadow. The trail crosses the dam at Coulter Reservoir, which also takes the old railroad grade across the East Fork Little Colorado River. Now the trail swings west and returns to parallel AZ 273 for a short distance. Then a sharp right and left turn (for a railroad) to the west signals the entrance to the shallow gorge containing the West Fork Little Colorado River. After crossing the highway and the small river, the trail contours east across the hillside just above the highway and arrives at Sheep Crossing trailhead at **10.3** miles.

The Apache Railroad Trail heads north briefly before crossing AZ 273 for the last time and turning northeast. It stays on the mesa just west of the river for a couple of miles, then turns north and descends off the mesa to cross a graveled forest road. After crossing Benny Creek on a bridge at **12.5** miles, the trail turns northwest and skirts the east side of Boardshack Knoll. As the trail passes the east side of White Mountain Reservoir, it crosses another graveled forest road at **13.9** miles. After crossing Hall Creek the trail continues generally northeast past Geneva Reservoir. After climbing through the low cliffs of a small bluff at **17.1** miles, the trail turns almost west, heading directly toward forested Big Cienega Mountain. Once close to the base of the mountain, the trail turns northwest again. As it approaches the 260 trailhead, the old Cienega ski area, long since closed, is visible to your left on the northeast slopes of Big Cienega Mountain. The trail ends at the Big Cienega trailhead at the north base of the mountain, marked by a tall red-and-white microwave tower.

GOING FARTHER
Although there are almost unlimited cross-country hiking possibilities in the wide-open alpine meadows, the main connecting trails are the East Baldy Trail starting from East Baldy trailhead, and the West Baldy Trail starting from Sheep Crossing trailhead. (See hikes #51 and #50 in this guide.)

50. West Baldy Trail

RATING	🚶 🚶 🚶 🚶 🚶
DISTANCE	14.2 miles round-trip
HIKING TIME	8 hours
ELEVATION GAIN	2,160 feet
HIGH POINT	11,420 feet
EFFORT	Prepare to Perspire
BEST SEASON	Summer, fall
WATER	West Fork Little Colorado River
PERMITS/CONTACT	None/Apache-Sitgreaves National Forests, (928) 333-4301, www.fs.usda.gov/asnf
MAPS	USGS Mount Baldy, Big Lake North; USFS Mount Baldy Wilderness
NOTES	Leashed dogs welcome. The upper portion of the trail has been rerouted and is not shown correctly on the topo map. The Fort Apache Indian Reservation, which borders the national forest along the summit of Mount Baldy, is closed to all access. Hikers have been fined and had their gear confiscated for trespassing.

THE HIKE

This popular hike is one of the classics in Arizona's high country, and follows the headwaters of the West Fork Little Colorado River, a beautiful alpine trout stream, and leads to a point near the summit of Mount Baldy. A short cross-country stroll leads to the bald high point of Arizona's second-highest mountain.

GETTING THERE

From Springerville, drive approximately 20 miles west on AZ 260 and turn left on AZ 273. Drive 8.7 miles to Sheep Crossing trailhead, on the right. Elevation 9,247 feet, GPS coordinates N33°57.942'; W109°29.994'

THE TRAIL

From Sheep Crossing trailhead, follow the West Baldy Trail southwest along the ridge above AZ 273 and the shallow gorge containing the small river. After passing the original trailhead and campground area,

The West Baldy Trail wanders through beautiful alpine meadows in the headwaters of the Little Colorado River.

now closed, the trail drops down next to the river, which it follows southwest up the open valley. At **1.2** miles, the Connector Trail comes in from the left; stay right on the West Fork Trail.

After a pleasant stretch of easy walking at a gentle gradient along the headwaters valley of the river, the trail enters dense forest and starts the final ascent of the mountain at **3.2** miles. A few switchbacks lead up through volcanic cliffs and finally onto the long summit ridge. The trail skirts just inside the tree line on the east side of the ridge, and meets the East Baldy Trail at **6.8** miles.

To hike to the summit, turn right and walk past a yellow national forest boundary sign (which is located incorrectly—the boundary is on the west side of the summit ridge, not the east) and into the meadow on the summit ridge. Stay on the crest of the ridge and walk south along an informal trail to the highest point of the ridge, labeled "Mount Baldy" on the topo map. *Do not continue north beyond the high point, and do not attempt to hike north to Baldy Peak.* The south end of the summit ridge and Baldy Peak are within the Fort Apache Indian Reservation. Rangers patrol the reservation boundary from a logging road just below the summit to the southeast, and you *will* be caught.

The highest point of the Mount Baldy ridge is actually slightly higher than Baldy Peak, even though it does not have a benchmarked elevation. The Indian reservation boundary runs along the west side of the

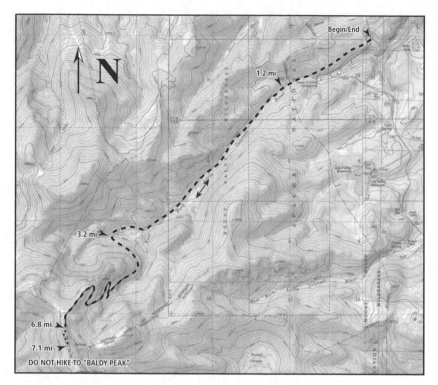

ridge, about 50 feet below the crest, as marked by small aluminum survey markers. So there is no reason to hike to Baldy Peak. If you are approached by an Apache ranger while on the summit ridge east of the survey markers, point out the markers to the ranger and explain that you are still in the national forest and are completely legal.

GOING FARTHER
You can do a fine loop hike over the summit of Mount Baldy by continuing on the East Fork Trail and then using the Connector Trail to return to Sheep Crossing trailhead. (See hike #51 in this guide.)

51. East Baldy Trail

RATING	🚶 🚶 🚶 🚶 🚶
DISTANCE	12.4 miles round-trip
HIKING TIME	8 hours
ELEVATION GAIN	2,025 feet
HIGH POINT	11,420 feet
EFFORT	Prepare to Perspire
BEST SEASON	Summer, fall
WATER	East Fork Little Colorado River
PERMITS/CONTACT	None/Apache-Sitgreaves National Forests, (928) 333-4301, www.fs.usda.gov/asnf
MAPS	USGS Big Lake North, Mount Baldy; USFS Mount Baldy Wilderness
NOTES	Leashed dogs welcome. The portion of the trail on the east ridge of Mount Baldy has been rerouted and is not shown correctly on the topo map. The Fort Apache Indian Reservation, which borders the national forest along the summit of Mount Baldy, is closed to all access. Hikers have been fined and had their gear confiscated for trespassing.

THE HIKE

This trail starts out along the East Fork Little Colorado River and climbs to a point near the bald summit of Mount Baldy, the state's second-highest mountain. It is a great alternative to the popular West Baldy Trail.

GETTING THERE

From Springerville, drive approximately 20 miles west on AZ 260 and turn left on AZ 273. Drive 12 miles to East Baldy trailhead, on the right. Elevation 9,391 feet, GPS coordinates N33°55.807'; W109°29.462'

THE TRAIL

From the trailhead, follow the East Baldy Trail as it heads generally west along the north bank of the East Fork Little Colorado River, a small alpine trout stream at this point close to the river's headwaters. After meandering through the open meadow and past small stands of fir and

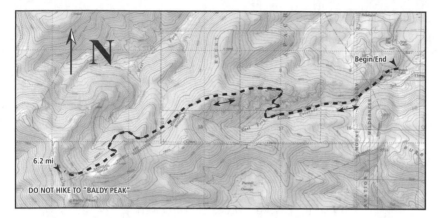

spruce, the trail abruptly turns right and climbs out of the valley to the north. Switchbacks lead through a break in some impressive volcanic cliffs and bring the trail to the top of the long east ridge of Mount Baldy. Once at the top, the trail turns west and climbs the ridge. At first the trail is near the ridge crest and this section offers some fine views of Mount Baldy to the west and the remainder of the White Mountains in the other direction. Eventually the trail drops below the crest of the ridge and stays in the dense forest on its north side. This section of the trail has been rerouted to remain completely in the national forest. The trail finally climbs to a point on the east side of the Mount Baldy summit ridge just at tree line, and meets the West Baldy Trail at **6.2** miles.

GOING FARTHER
To hike to the summit of Mount Baldy from this point without trespassing on the Fort Apache Indian Reservation, see the West Baldy Trail (hike #50 in this guide).

A loop hike can be done either direction by using the Connector Trail or the Apache Railroad Trail to connect the East and West Baldy Trails near their trailheads. The Connector Trail is not shown on the topo map, but starts at the East Baldy trailhead and heads north-northwest along the wilderness boundary, skirts west of Lee Reservoir, and meets the West Baldy Trail 1.2 miles west of Sheep Crossing trailhead. The trail is 2.6 miles long.

The Apache Railroad Trail is across AZ 273 from Gabaldon Campground, just east of the East Baldy trailhead. It is 5 miles from here to Sheep Crossing trailhead.

52. KP Creek

RATING	🚶 🚶 🚶 🚶
DISTANCE	20.2-mile loop
HIKING TIME	12 hours or 2 days
ELEVATION GAIN	2,720 feet
HIGH POINT	9,280 feet
EFFORT	Prepare to Perspire
BEST SEASON	Summer, fall
WATER	Willow Spring, Upper Grant Creek, Lower Grant Creek, Mud Spring, KP Creek
PERMITS/CONTACT	None/Apache-Sitgreaves National Forests, (928) 333-4301, www.fs.usda.gov/asnf
MAPS	USGS Strayhorse, Bear Mountain, Hannagan Meadow; USFS Blue Range Wilderness
NOTES	Leashed dogs welcome. You may encounter horses. Much of this area has been repeatedly burned in wildfires, including the Wallow Fire in 2011. Expect areas of deadfall on the trails.

THE HIKE

The "Blue," as the area drained by eastern Arizona's Blue River is known by locals, is a system of deep canyons cut into the eastern end of the Mogollon Rim. This hike starts in alpine fir and spruce forest and loops through deep canyons and down to pinyon-juniper woodland before returning to the 9,000-foot rim at the start.

GETTING THERE

From Alpine, drive 24.2 miles south on U.S. 191 to KP Rim trailhead, on the left. Elevation 9,078 feet, GPS coordinates N33°36.860'; W109°19.685'

THE TRAIL

Leave the KP Rim trailhead on the KP Rim Trail, which heads east along the north rim of KP Creek. One of the few good things about the burned forest is that it improves the view of the 1,000-foot canyon containing KP Creek. At **1.9** miles, turn left on the unnamed connecting trail that heads northwest. (The Steeple Trail continues straight ahead.)

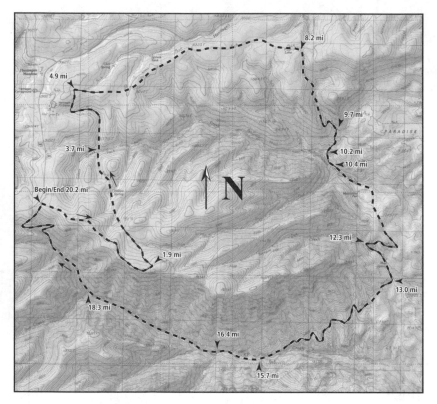

Follow the connecting trail as it cuts across the heads of several major drainages and climbs over the intervening ridges. In the first drainage, an unnamed trail goes right; stay left on the connecting trail. In the third drainage, you'll pass Willow Spring in a meadow. The fourth drainage is the head of Grant Creek at **3.7** miles, where the Grant Creek Trail goes right, down the creek. Stay left and follow the connecting trail up a side drainage to the north and west to meet the Paradise Trail at **4.9** miles.

Turn right on the Paradise Trail and follow it east across the broad ridge north of Grant Creek and its tributaries. At P Bar Lake, which is just a shallow pond at mile **8.2**, turn right to stay on the Paradise Trail and descend south down a canyon. At **9.7** miles, turn right and continue the descent into Grant Creek. Here, at **10.2** miles, the Grant Creek Trail comes in on the right. Continue straight ahead, passing another trail that also turns right, at **10.4** miles, and heads up an unnamed tributary of Grant Creek.

The trail heads southeast and passes around the east side of Moonshine Park, climbs over a ridge, then turns sharply west to meet the Steeple

Creek Trail at **12.3** miles. Turn left on the Steeple Creek Trail, follow it southeast past Mud Spring, and meet the KP Creek Trail at mile **13.0**.

Turn right on the KP Creek Trail and follow it across the north slopes of KP Creek Canyon and down into KP Creek at **15.7** miles, where a trail forks left. Stay on the KP Creek Trail and follow it up KP Creek to another trail junction at **16.4** miles. At **18.3** miles, leave the KP Creek Trail and turn right on the North KP Trail, which climbs up an unnamed tributary to end at the KP Rim trailhead.

GOING FARTHER
The Blue has an extensive network of trails covering most of this vast wilderness. The USFS Blue Range Wilderness map gives the best overview of the trail system.

53. Bear Wallow Trail

RATING	🚶 🚶 🚶 🚶
DISTANCE	14.9 miles round-trip
HIKING TIME	10 hours or 2 days
ELEVATION GAIN	3,070 feet
HIGH POINT	9,730 feet
EFFORT	Prepare to Perspire
BEST SEASON	Summer, fall
WATER	Bear Wallow Creek
PERMITS/CONTACT	None/Apache-Sitgreaves National Forests, (928) 333-4301, www.fs.usda.gov/asnf
MAPS	USGS Baldy Bill Point
NOTES	Leashed dogs welcome. You may encounter horses. The upper end of Bear Wallow Creek was burned in 2011 by the gigantic Wallow Fire, which was started by an abandoned campfire in the upper end of Bear Wallow Canyon. Fortunately the fire burned to the northeast, sparing most of this trail.

THE HIKE

This pleasant walk descends into Bear Wallow Creek and follows the creek westward through fir, aspen, and pine forest to the national forest boundary.

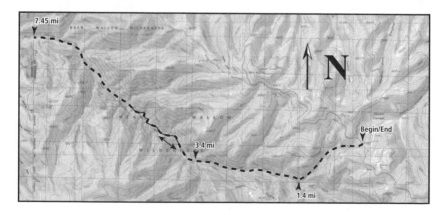

Groves of quaking aspen add a splash of fall color along upper Bear Wallow Creek.

GETTING THERE

From Alpine, drive 27.4 miles south on U.S. 191 and turn right on Forest Road 25. Drive 3.2 miles to the Bear Wallow trail, on the left. The access roads are dirt and may be impassable during winter or wet weather. Elevation 8,729 feet, GPS coordinates N33°36.197'; W109°23.839'

THE TRAIL

From the trailhead, follow the Bear Wallow Trail southwest down a drainage. At **1.4** miles, the trail reaches the North Fork Bear Wallow Creek and turns downstream. At **3.4** miles, the South Fork Bear Wallow Creek and Trail join from the left; stay right and continue on the Bear Wallow Creek Trail west, downstream along Bear Wallow Creek. Your hike ends at a fence marking the national forest/Indian reservation boundary at **7.45** miles—the reservation is closed to the public.

Tall saguaro cactus are the signature plant of the Sonoran Desert.

PHOENIX AREA

The greater Phoenix area is located in the northern Sonoran Desert, a relatively lush desert with a rich mixture of desert cactus, shrubs, and small trees. After a wet winter, if conditions are right, the desert blooms with a spring wildflower show that has to been seen to be believed. The barren-looking desert soil hides billions of seeds just waiting for a good year. Among the showiest blossoms are the cactus flowers, which range from garlands of white to deep red flowers that almost seem to glow with inner light.

Although it's too hot to hike in these desert mountains during the summer, the weather in fall, winter, and early spring is delightful.

Within the city and around its edges are a number of regional county parks, all of which have extensive trail networks. In addition, there are several wilderness areas and national monuments near the city, which have trails. The hikes in this section barely scratch the surface of this wonderful desert hiking area.

PHOENIX AREA

54. Go John Trail

RATING	🚶 🚶 🚶 🚶
DISTANCE	4.5 miles
HIKING TIME	3 hours
ELEVATION GAIN	410 feet
HIGH POINT	2,545 feet
EFFORT	Easy Walk
BEST SEASON	Fall–spring
WATER	Picnic areas
PERMITS/CONTACT	Park entrance fee/Cave Creek Regional Park, (623) 465-0431, www.maricopa.gov/parks/cave_creek
MAPS	USGS Cave Creek. The trail is not shown on the topo.
NOTES	Dogs on leashes 6 feet or less welcome. You may encounter mountain bikes on the trail.

THE HIKE

This trail loops through Sonoran Desert foothills in Cave Creek Regional Park, through stands of saguaro and cholla cactus. The north end of the loop provides distant views of the New River Mountains.

GETTING THERE

From Carefree at the junction of Carefree Highway and Scottsdale Road, drive 4.9 miles west on Carefree Highway and turn right on 32nd Street. Drive north, enter Cave Creek Regional Park, and continue to the Go John trailhead. Elevation 2,119 feet, GPS coordinates N33°49.942'; W112°00.096'

THE TRAIL

From the trailhead, head north on the Go John Trail, which soon climbs over a low pass and descends a drainage to the north. Numerous informal trails branch off, generally to the left; stay right, or on the most used trail, if you have any doubt.

At 1.5 miles, the Go John Trail leaves the ravine and heads east over a low saddle. After following a drainage for a short distance, the trail

After a wet winter, the Sonoran Desert can be a solid carpet of wildflowers.

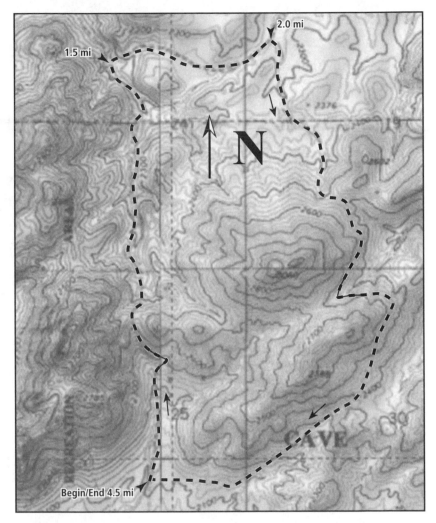

turns sharply right at mile **2.0** and works its way up gentle desert slopes to cross a saddle northeast of Peak 3060. It then contours around a ridge and turns southwest to cross another saddle before descending along the hillside back to the trailhead.

55. Pass Mountain Trail

RATING	🚶 🚶 🚶 🚶
DISTANCE	6.5-mile loop
HIKING TIME	4 hours
ELEVATION GAIN	910 feet
HIGH POINT	2,790 feet
EFFORT	Moderate Workout
BEST SEASON	Fall–spring
WATER	Picnic areas
PERMITS/CONTACT	None/Usery Mountain Regional Park, (480) 984-0032, www.maricopa.gov/parks/usery
MAPS	USGS Apache Junction
NOTES	Dogs on leashes 6 feet or less welcome. You may encounter mountain bikes on the trail.

THE HIKE

The backside of this loop hike around Pass Mountain in Usery Mountain Park features expansive vistas of the Goldfield Mountains and the southern Mazatzal Mountains, and provides a surprising wilderness feel, considering the park's closeness to the growing city of Mesa.

GETTING THERE

From Mesa at McDowell Road and Usery Pass Road, drive 1.5 miles north on Usery Pass Road and turn right into Usery Mountain Park. Stay left and continue 1.6 miles to the Pass Mountain trailhead and horse staging area. Elevation 1,912 feet, GPS coordinates N33°28.057'; W111°36.436'

THE TRAIL

From the horse staging area/trailhead, head east 0.1 mile to a trail junction and turn left on the Pass Mountain Trail. Continue north along the slopes at the base of Pass Mountain, passing the Wind Cave trailhead and crossing the Wind Cave Trail. The Pass Mountain Trail continues to climb steadily to the north, then circles around the north slopes of the mountain. As the gradual climb continues along the northeast slopes of Pass Mountain, you're treated to a succession of sweeping views of the wild country to the northeast. At **3.6** miles, the trail crosses through the

Teddy-bear cholla and saguaro cactus are plentiful along the Pass Mountain Trail.

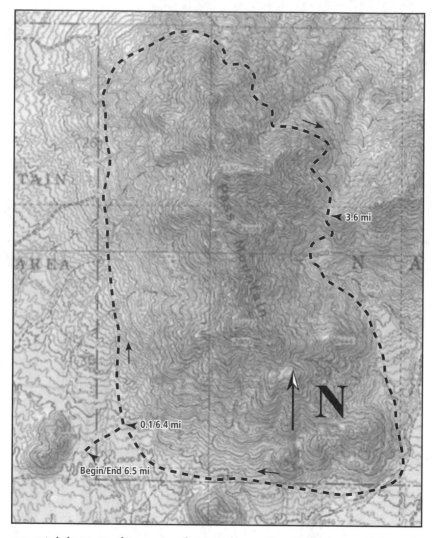

mountain's namesake pass, and starts descending the slopes to the south. A short, steep section of trail leads to a gentler descent along the east slopes of the mountain and around the south side. Stay right at the junction with the two ends of the Cat Pass Trail, which loops around a small hill at the south end of Pass Mountain. At **6.4** miles, turn left to return to the trailhead.

56. Margies Cove Trail

RATING	🚶 🚶 🚶 🚶
DISTANCE	9.0 miles round-trip
HIKING TIME	5 hours
ELEVATION GAIN	465 feet
HIGH POINT	1,560 feet
EFFORT	Moderate Workout
BEST SEASON	Fall–spring
WATER	None
PERMITS/CONTACT	None/Sonoran Desert National Monument, (623) 580-5500, www.blm.gov/az/st/en/prog/ blm_special_areas/natmon/son_des.html
MAPS	USGS Margies Peak, Cotton Center SE
NOTES	Leashed dogs welcome

THE HIKE

The Margies Cove Trail is a delightful hike through open desert hills in the Sonoran Desert National Monument. Although a longish day hike, the walking is very easy.

GETTING THERE

From Interstate 10 at AZ 85 west of Phoenix, drive 20.5 miles south and turn left on a dirt road. Continue 3.8 miles and turn right. Drive 0.4 mile

The Margies Cove Trail wanders across Sonoran Desert plains in the North Maricopa Mountains.

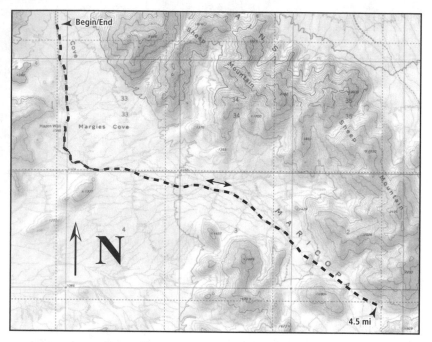

to the Margies Cove trailhead at the end of the road. The access roads
are dirt and may be impassable during winter or wet weather. Elevation
1,156 feet, GPS coordinates N33°08.142'; W112°35.029'

THE TRAIL
Head south through the broad flat of Margies Cove. Shortly after the trail
passes the remains of Hazan Well, it turns southeast and heads toward
the base of the Maricopa Mountains. Your turnaround point is the junction with the Brittlebrush Trail at **4.5** miles.

GOING FARTHER
Although it's possible to follow the Margies Cove Trail farther to its end
at the East Margies trailhead, or take the Brittlebrush Trail south to the
Brittlebrush trailhead, the access roads are currently closed, so a car
shuttle is not possible. Check with the national monument for updates.

57. Table Top Trail

RATING	🚶 🚶 🚶 🚶
DISTANCE	6.5 miles round-trip
HIKING TIME	4 hours
ELEVATION GAIN	2,050 feet
HIGH POINT	4,356 feet
EFFORT	Moderate Workout
BEST SEASON	Fall–spring
WATER	None
PERMITS/CONTACT	None/Sonoran Desert National Monument, (623) 580-5500, www.blm.gov/az/st/en/prog/ blm_special_areas/natmon/son_des.html
MAPS	USGS Little Table Top
NOTES	Leashed dogs welcome

THE HIKE

Another fine hike in the newly created Sonoran Desert National Monument, this one takes you to the summit of Table Top Mountain for a view of an unspoiled section of the desert.

GETTING THERE

From near Casa Grande at the junction of Interstate 10 and Interstate 8, drive 33.5 miles west on I-8 and exit at Vekol Valley Road. Turn left and drive 11.3 miles south and turn left. Drive 4.7 miles to the Table Top trailhead and the end of the road. The access roads are dirt and may be impassable during winter or wet weather. Elevation 2,304 feet, GPS coordinates N32°42.998'; W112°09.525'

THE TRAIL

Heading generally northeast, the first half of the trail follows old roads. About 0.5 mile up the desert valley, the trail climbs onto a low ridge and follows it toward Table Top, which is visible ahead. When it reaches the foot of the mountain at mile 2.0, the trail narrows and climbs directly up a steep ridge. A few short switchbacks lead to the south summit plateau.

Saguaro cactus use its fleshy interior to store water between infrequent rains.

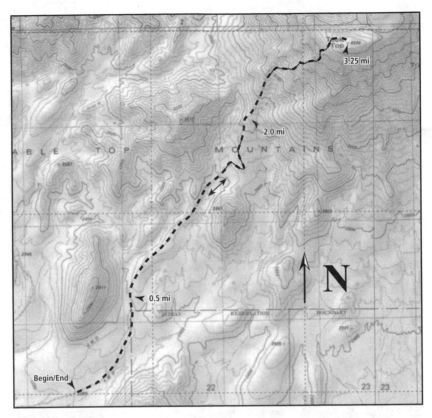

GOING FARTHER

There are actually two summits, both labeled "Table Top" on the topo map. The trail ends at the south summit, but it is an easy cross-country walk of less than 0.5 mile to the north summit, which is 17 feet higher according to the topo.

An isolated aspen grove in the Rincon Mountains in Saguaro National Park.

TUCSON AREA

Tucson is surrounded by three mountain ranges that provide nearby recreation with a great deal of variety. On the west, the Tucson Mountains are a desert range rising to over 5,000 feet and protected as part of Saguaro National Park. The park and the adjoining Tucson Mountain Park administered by the county offer miles of desert hiking among the giant saguaro cactus, the signature plant of the Sonoran Desert.

On the east edge of Tucson, the Rincon Mountains rise from desert foothills to over 8,000 feet, and the summit area features granite outcrops and pinnacles set in a mixed forest. The Rincon Mountains are part of the Saguaro National Park and have a trail system that covers the range from the desert foothills to the summits.

The Santa Catalina Mountains rise abruptly from the north edge of the city to over 9,000 feet. Unlike most of the isolated mountain ranges of southern Arizona, the Catalinas are a complex range with two main crests: the Front Range visible from Tucson, and the Mount Lemmon crest to the north. Although a paved highway leads to the top of the mountain, much of the southern and western portion of the mountain is wilderness. Hiking the trail network here is a strenuous undertaking due to the large elevation range, but that same elevation range allows for year-round hiking.

TUCSON AREA

58. Wilderness of Rocks

RATING	🚶 🚶 🚶 🚶
DISTANCE	3.1-mile loop
HIKING TIME	2 hours
ELEVATION GAIN	700 feet
HIGH POINT	8,130 feet
EFFORT	Moderate Workout
BEST SEASON	Summer, fall
WATER	Marshall Gulch, Huntsman Spring
PERMITS/CONTACT	Mount Lemmon entrance fee/Coronado National Forest, (520) 388-8300, www.fs.usda.gov/coronado
MAPS	USGS Mount Lemmon; USFS Pusch Ridge Wilderness
NOTES	Leashed dogs welcome

THE HIKE

This fine loop traverses a variety of forest types due to the changing exposure and slopes. It also offers an overview of the Wilderness of Rocks, a portion of the Santa Catalina Mountains in the Pusch Ridge Wilderness, which is distinguished by its rugged granite rock formations.

GETTING THERE

From Tucson at Tanque Verde Road and Catalina Highway, drive 29.3 miles north on Catalina Highway and drive into Summerhaven. Continue 1.3 miles south to the end of the road at Marshall Gulch Picnic Area. Elevation 7,442 feet, GPS coordinates N32°25.681'; W110°45.333'

THE TRAIL

Start out on the Marshall Gulch Trail, which climbs directly west up Marshall Gulch. At **0.5** mile you'll pass Huntsman Spring. Continue up the gulch on the trail to a five-way trail junction in a saddle at **1.3** miles. Turn left on the Aspen Trail, which heads south through a saddle and then begins contouring around the southwest slopes of Marshall Peak.

At **1.7** miles, you can leave the trail to the southwest and walk less than 0.1 mile to the far side of a hill for great views of the Wilderness of Rocks.

The remote fastnesses of the Wilderness of Rocks is home to varied wildlife, including mountain lions.

Returning to the Aspen Trail, continue east through a saddle and then follow the trail down the east slopes of Marshall Peak. A short final descent into Sabino Canyon leads back to the trailhead.

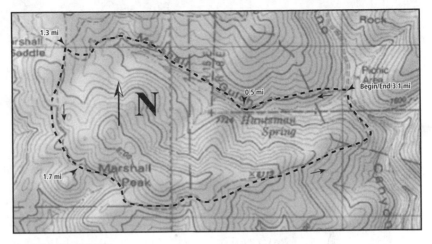

GOING FARTHER

The five-way trail junction at **1.3** miles connects to several trails that lead deep into the Wilderness of Rocks. Study of the topo maps shows many possibilities for long day hikes and extended backpack trips. One caution—water sources are highly seasonal in the Santa Catalinas, and the best time for backpacking is in the spring after a wet winter assures plenty of water. See the Pusch Ridge Wilderness Map for an overview.

59. Finger Rock Trail

RATING	🚶 🚶 🚶 🚶 🚶
DISTANCE	7.8 miles round-trip
HIKING TIME	7 hours
ELEVATION GAIN	4,010 feet
HIGH POINT	7,134 feet
EFFORT	Knee-Punishing
BEST SEASON	Spring, fall
WATER	Seasonal at Finger Rock Spring
PERMITS/CONTACT	None/Coronado National Forest, (520) 388-8300, www.fs.usda.gov/coronado
MAPS	USGS Tucson North; USFS Pusch Ridge Wilderness
NOTES	Leashed dogs welcome

THE HIKE

The elevation gain on this hike is comparable to that in the Grand Canyon, and the scenery is nearly as dramatic. The long climb takes you to the top of Mount Kimball, a prominent summit in the Front Range of the Santa Catalina Mountains.

GETTING THERE

From Interstate 10 in Tucson, exit onto Orange Grove Road and drive east 6.7 miles. Turn right on Skyline Road and drive 1.7 miles. Turn left onto Alvernon Way and continue 1 mile north to Finger Rock trailhead at the end of the road. Parking is limited. Elevation 3,115 feet, GPS coordinates N32°20.244'; W110°54.650'

THE TRAIL

Follow the Finger Rock Trail north along the narrow right-of-way. Stay on the trail and respect the surrounding private property. The trail emerges onto the Coronado National Forest as it enters the mouth of Finger Rock Canyon, which is named for the rock pinnacle on the western skyline of the canyon.

After about 1.0 mile the Finger Rock Trail leaves the bed of the canyon and climbs up the east slopes. As the trail passes above the 4,000-foot

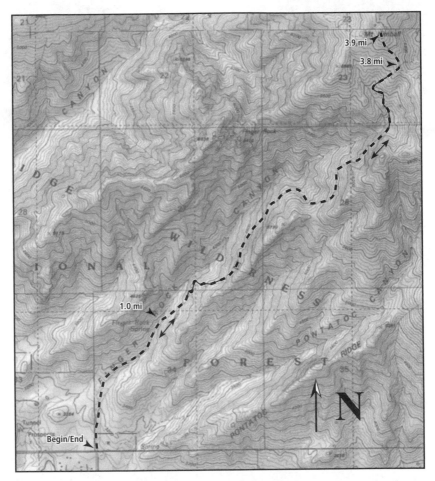

contour and enters the head of Finger Rock Canyon, it leaves the desert behind and enters pinyon-juniper woodland.

At **3.8** miles the trail reaches a saddle. Turn left here and ascend 0.1 mile to the summit of Mount Kimball.

The Santa Catalina Mountains are one of many isolated mountain ranges in southeastern Arizona that rise like green islands in a sea of desert. Reaching as high as 10,000 feet in elevation, the tops of these mountains are forested with ponderosa and Apache pine, Douglas fir, blue spruce, and quaking aspen. They offer a cool summer refuge from the scorching desert below.

Finger Rock Canyon is named for this prominent pinnacle on the skyline.

GOING FARTHER

The Finger Rock Trail connects to the Pima Canyon Trail, which could be used for an extended hike with a car shuttle to the Pima Canyon trail-head. Other trails connect to an extensive trail system in the Pusch Ridge Wilderness. See the Pusch Ridge Wilderness map for an overview.

60. Mica Mountain

RATING	🚶 🚶 🚶 🚶 🚶
DISTANCE	22.7 miles round-trip
HIKING TIME	2 or 3 days
ELEVATION GAIN	5,920 feet
HIGH POINT	8,664 feet
EFFORT	Knee-Punishing
BEST SEASON	Spring
WATER	Manning Camp Spring (1.1-mile side trip)
PERMITS/CONTACT	Permit required for backcountry camping/Saguaro National Park, (520) 733-5153, www.nps.gov/sagu
MAPS	USGS Tanque Verde Peak, Mica Mountain; Trails Illustrated Saguaro National Park
NOTES	Dogs prohibited on trails in the national park. Black bears are common in the Rincon Mountains. Backpackers must camp at one of the designated backcountry campgrounds and store their food and all scented items including toiletries and sunscreen in one of the steel bear boxes provided. Since there is only one permanent water source along this long hike, it is best done in the spring after a wet winter, when there will be seasonal creeks and springs.

THE HIKE

This long hike takes you to the top of Mica Peak in the Rincon Mountains, one of the few major sky island ranges that does not have a road to the top.

GETTING THERE

From Interstate 10 in Tucson, exit at Speedway Blvd and drive east 17.4 miles to the Douglas Spring trailhead at the end of the road. Elevation 2,746 feet, GPS coordinates N32°14.124'; W110°41.218'

At 8,264 feet, Rincon Peak dominates the southern Rincon Mountains.

THE TRAIL

Follow the Douglas Spring Trail east from the trailhead. Several other trails join from the right in the first 1.0 mile, part of an extensive foothills trail system; stay left on the Douglas Spring Trail at each junction. After leaving the flat desert forest of saguaro cactus, the trail turns southeast and starts the long climb up a ridge. After turning east and passing between two hills, you'll encounter a side trail going right at **2.3** miles. This 0.2-mile trail leads to Bridal Wreath Falls, a seasonal waterfall that is most likely to be flowing in the spring.

Back on the Douglas Spring Trail, continue east as the trail again begins to climb, leaving the Sonoran Desert behind and ascending into high desert grassland. The trail continues in an easterly direction until it reaches Douglas Camp Spring at **5.5** miles. This spot is an ideal destination for a day hike. For backpackers, this is a designated backcountry campground and a pleasant spot in the spring when there is usually water.

The trail now turns to the south and starts climbing directly toward Tanque Verde Ridge, the long west ridge of Mica Mountain. At **7.3** miles, the Douglas Spring Trail ends at Cow Head Saddle, a four-way trail intersection. Turn left on the Cow Head Saddle Trail and hike east. The

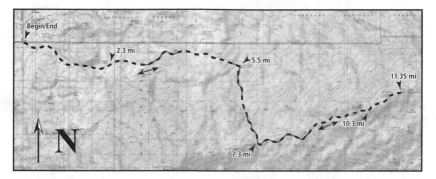

trail continues a steady climb and at **10.3** miles, you'll reach another junction, just southeast of Helens Dome. Turn right on the Manning Camp Trail and follow it just 0.2 mile to the Fire Loop Trail.

Manning Camp has the only reliable spring in the summit area and is also a backcountry campground. The camp and spring are 0.5 mile down the Manning Camp Trail, on the right.

To continue to the top of Mica Mountain, turn left on the Fire Loop Trail and continue up the ridge to the east. The summit area is a fine mix of granite domes and boulders, ponderosa pine, aspen, and Douglas fir. At Spud Rock, another trail comes in from the right; stay left on the Fire Loop Trail and continue to Mica Mountain, the summit of the Rincon Mountains. A fire lookout tower once stood on this 8,664-foot summit, but only the foundation remains. Views are somewhat limited by the forest.

GOING FARTHER

The Rincon Mountain district of Saguaro National Park has many miles of trails. For those staying at Manning Camp and using it as a base, a network of trails loops through the granite dome country surrounding Mica Mountain.

An extensive network of shorter trails covers the desert foothill area between the Douglas Spring trailhead and the Cactus Forest Loop Drive. There are also two trails that climb the east side of the mountain from the Miller Creek and Turkey Creek trailheads. These trails give you access to the network of trails around Mica Mountain and also to Rincon Peak at the southern end of the range.

61. Signal Hill Trail

RATING	🚶 🚶 🚶
DISTANCE	0.5 mile round-trip
HIKING TIME	30 minutes
ELEVATION GAIN	50 feet
HIGH POINT	2,470 feet
EFFORT	Stroll in the Park
BEST SEASON	Fall–spring
WATER	None
PERMITS/CONTACT	None/Saguaro National Park, (520) 733-5158, www.nps.gov/sagu
MAPS	USGS Avra; Trails Illustrated Saguaro National Park
NOTES	Dogs prohibited on trails in the national park. Backcountry camping is not allowed in the Tucson Mountain District of the park.

THE HIKE

Although short, this nice walk takes you to the top of a rocky hill with prehistoric petroglyphs and a fine view of the Tucson Mountains.

GETTING THERE

From the Red Hills Visitor Center, turn right on Kinney Road. After 2.1 miles, turn right onto Sandario Road. Drive 0.2 mile and turn right on Golden Gate Road, then drive 1.2 miles to the Signal Hill Road and turn left. Continue 0.4 mile to the Signal Hill Picnic Area. Elevation 2,429 feet, GPS coordinates N32°17.388'; W111°12.578'

THE TRAIL

Starting from the picnic area and trailhead, follow the easy trail north and then around the east side of Signal Hill to the summit. There are several examples of petroglyphs, art that is pecked into the rock, on boulders around the summit area. The vast saguaro "forest" surrounds you, with countless thousands of these giant cacti covering every hillside and desert flat.

Saguaro cacti, the signature plants of the northern Sonoran Desert, are water-savers. That is, they use a widespread but shallow root system

As seen on Signal Hill, petroglyphs are ancient rock art pecked into the rock.

to take advantage of infrequent desert rains to rapidly absorb moisture and store it in their fleshy interior. Unlike trees, saguaros have no woody core. As a glance at the skeleton of a dead saguaro will show you, the cactus has an outer framework of ribs surrounding the succulent core. This allows the plant to expand and contract in accordion-like folds, depending on the moisture it contains. The skin of the plant is tough and waxy, which helps to limit moisture loss in the extremely low desert humidity.

Saguaros bloom in the late spring with a showy crown of fragrant white flowers. Each plant produces millions of tiny black seeds, most of which are eaten by birds and other wildlife, or fail to land on a suitable spot. The most successful saguaro seedlings are those that germinate under a palo verde tree. This "nurse" tree protects the young cactus from extremes of cold and sunlight. As you walk through the desert, you'll see young saguaros, only a foot or two tall, growing under their nurse trees. Since saguaros live much longer than palo verde trees, mature saguaros are usually found on their own.

GOING FARTHER
There are many other trails suitable for easy to strenuous day hikes in the Tucson Mountain District of the national park, and also in the adjoining Tucson Mountain Park. See the Trails Illustrated map for an overview.

62. Hugh Norris Trail

RATING	🚶 🚶 🚶 🚶 🚶
DISTANCE	8.2 miles round-trip
HIKING TIME	5 hours
ELEVATION GAIN	2,110 feet
HIGH POINT	4,687 feet
EFFORT	Prepare to Perspire
BEST SEASON	Fall–spring
WATER	None
PERMITS/CONTACT	None/Saguaro National Park, (520) 733-5158, www.nps.gov/sagu
MAPS	USGS Avra; Trails Illustrated Saguaro National Park
NOTES	Dogs prohibited on trails in the national park. Backcountry camping is not allowed in the Tucson Mountain District of the park.

THE HIKE

A beautiful but strenuous hike that climbs along a desert ridge and offers views of the surrounding Tucson Mountains. The hike leads to Wasson Peak, at 4,687 feet the highest point in the Tucson Mountains.

GETTING THERE

From the Red Hills Visitor Center, turn right and drive northwest 1.7 miles on Kinney Road. Turn right on Bajada Loop Drive and drive 0.8 mile to the Hugh Norris trailhead. Elevation 2,576 feet, GPS coordinates N32°16.353'; W111°12.203'

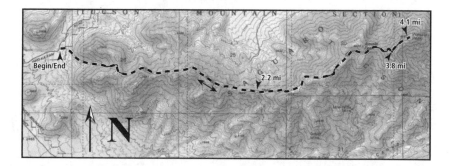

The last few yards of trail to the summit of Wasson Peak traverses a high desert grassland.

THE TRAIL

Follow the Hugh Norris Trail east into a canyon, which the trail climbs to gain a saddle, then works its way around the north side of a rocky hill to finally gain the crest of the ridge. The trail stays more or less on the top of the ridge all the way to Wasson Peak.

At **2.2** miles, cross the Sendero Esperanza Trail in a saddle and continue east up the ridge on the Hugh Norris Trail. After the trail crosses the south slopes of Amole Peak, it meets the Sweetwater Trail at **3.8** miles. Turn left and walk the last 0.3 mile to the summit.

You'll notice that saguaro cactus disappears from the highest part of this hike, and also grows lower on west- and south-facing slopes than on north- and east-facing slopes. That's because saguaro cactus can't take prolonged freezing temperatures, which are the upper limits of its range. Although snow occasionally falls in the highest elevations of the saguaro forest, it never stays on the ground for more than a few hours.

GOING FARTHER

You can hike the Sendero Esperanza Trail north from the junction at 2.2 miles to a trailhead on the Golden Gate Road, or hike the same trail south and connect with the King Canyon Trail and several other trails.

63. King Canyon Trail

RATING	🚶 🚶 🚶 🚶
DISTANCE	6.1 miles round-trip
HIKING TIME	4 hours
ELEVATION GAIN	1,775 feet
HIGH POINT	4,687 feet
EFFORT	Prepare to Perspire
BEST SEASON	Fall–spring
WATER	None
PERMITS/CONTACT	None/Saguaro National Park, (520) 733-5158, www.nps.gov/sagu/
MAPS	USGS Brown Mountain, Avra; Trails Illustrated Saguaro National Park
NOTES	Dogs prohibited on trails in the national park. Backcountry camping is not allowed in the Tucson Mountain District of the park.

THE HIKE

This is an alternative and slightly shorter trail to the top of Wasson Peak that is not quite as scenic but also not nearly as crowded as the Hugh Norris Trail. The views from the summit are just as good no matter which trail you use to get there!

GETTING THERE

From the Red Hills Visitor Center, turn left on Kinney Road and drive 1.9 miles to the King Canyon/Gould Mine trailhead, on the left. Elevation 2,911 feet, GPS coordinates N32°14.857'; W111°10.127'

THE TRAIL

The King Canyon Trail heads northwest up its namesake canyon, following an old road with elaborate storm-work construction. The road was built for access to mines in the area, before it became a national park. Remains of the mines are visible on the south slopes of Amole Peak.

At **0.9 mile**, the Sendero Esperanza Trail branches left; stay right on the King Canyon Trail. Shortly beyond this junction, the trail climbs out of the wash on the left and starts working its way up the slopes north of

Saguaro cactus flowers usually only open at night during late spring, but during unseasonably cool weather the blossoms may remain open during the day.

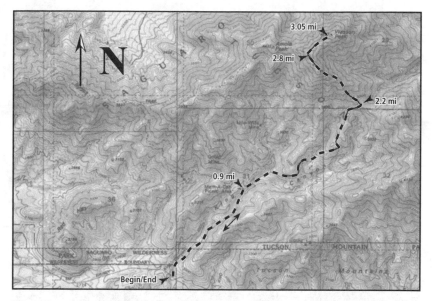

King Canyon. A final steep ascent up a ridge leads to a saddle at a trail junction at **2.2** miles. Turn left on the Sweetwater Trail and follow it up the steep ridge to the east. Your reward for this stiff climb is, of course, ever-better views of the rugged Tucson Mountains as well as Tucson itself to the east.

At **2.8** miles, turn right on the Hugh Norris Trail and hike to the summit of Wasson Peak.

The palo verde, Arizona's state tree, is common in the Sonoran Desert. The Spanish name means "green stick." In contrast to the saguaro and most other cacti, palo verde trees survive sustained dry periods in the desert by sending down long taproots to reach permanent water. A 10-foot-high tree may have a 50-foot taproot! Another survival strategy used by the palo verde is to drop its tiny leaves during dry periods and carry on photosynthesis using the chlorophyll in its green bark.

GOING FARTHER

A much shorter loop hike of 2.4 miles can be done by turning left on the Sendero Esperanza Trail, then left again on the Gould Mine Trail to return to the trailhead.

Sycamore Creek is a vital water source for wildlife in the Pajarita Wilderness.

SOUTHERN MOUNTAINS

Southeastern Arizona is known for its "sky island" ranges—isolated mountains that rise abruptly from the 4,000- to 5,000-foot valleys to over 10,000 feet. The valleys are high desert on the boundary between the Sonoran and Chihuahuan deserts, while the mountains are topped with ponderosa and Apache pine forest. The highest summits and north-facing slopes feature a beautiful mixed forest of pine, fir, spruce, and aspen. Intermediate elevations are a mix of small pinyon pine trees, juniper trees, and chaparral brush.

Some of the hikes in this section lead to forested mountain summits and others follow permanent streams through desert foothill canyons. Others wander through strange rock formations. In any case, there is a lot of fine hiking to do on the sky islands, and the elevation range makes this a year-round hiking area.

SOUTHERN MOUNTAINS

64. Aravaipa Canyon

RATING	🚶 🚶 🚶 🚶 🚶
DISTANCE	20.2 miles round-trip
HIKING TIME	2 to 4 days
ELEVATION GAIN	450 feet
HIGH POINT	3,070 feet
EFFORT	Moderate Workout
BEST SEASON	Spring–fall
WATER	Aravaipa Creek
PERMITS/CONTACT	Permit required for all access. East Aravaipa Canyon Wilderness, Klondyke Ranger Station, (928) 828-3380; West Aravaipa Canyon Wilderness, Brandenburg Ranger Station, (520) 357-6185; www.blm.gov/az/st/en/arolrsmain/aravaipa.html
MAPS	USGS Brandenburg Mountain, Booger Canyon
NOTES	Dogs prohibited. Access to each end of the canyon is through private property owned by The Nature Conservancy. Stay limit is three days/two nights. Popular dates fill up early, so it is advisable to get your permit online. The east trailhead is less popular than the west due to longer access roads.

THE HIKE

Aravaipa Canyon is one of the classic Arizona hikes. Although there is no trail, the walking is generally easy along the stream. Bring river sandals or mesh-topped amphibious hiking shoes—conventional hiking boots will be ruined in this canyon. The shady riparian vegetation and wildlife habitat are a delight, and there are several side canyons to explore.

GETTING THERE

To reach the Aravaipa West trailhead, from Winkelman, drive 10.7 miles south on AZ 77 and turn left on Aravaipa Road. Drive 12 miles east to the Aravaipa West trailhead. The access roads are dirt and may be impassable during winter or wet weather. Elevation 2,619 feet, GPS coordinates N32°54.192'; W110°33.996'

Aravaipa Creek supports a rich variety of wildlife along its riparian corridor.

To reach the Aravaipa East trailhead, from AZ 77 at U.S. 70 east of Globe, drive 59 miles east on U.S. 70 and turn right on Klondyke Road. Continue 24.5 miles and turn right on Aravaipa Canyon Road. Drive 17 miles to the Aravaipa East trailhead at the end of the road. The access roads are dirt and may be impassable during winter or wet weather. Elevation 3,094 feet, GPS coordinates N32°53.913'; W110°26.401'

THE TRAIL

As mentioned before, there is no trail. The hike follows the streambed for 10.1 miles from the west to the east trailhead.

Humans have used the Aravaipa Canyon area since at least 9,500 years ago. A well-preserved cliff dwelling is located 1.4 miles south of the east trailhead and was used by the Salado culture until about 1450. Other evidence of early use is scattered throughout the wilderness. Please obey the law and respect all prehistoric and historic artifacts by leaving them undisturbed.

During the middle of the 19th century, when southern Arizona became part of the United States, Aravaipa Canyon and the valley to the east were the home of the Aravaipa band of the Western Apache tribe. Fierce warriors, the Apache used Aravaipa Canyon as a route for their raids into Mexico.

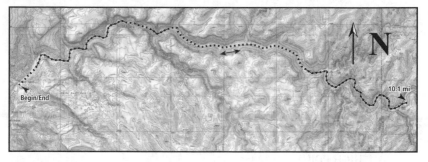

Riparian (streamside) areas such as Aravaipa Canyon are important wildlife habitats in Arizona, where free-flowing streams have become rare because of diversion and groundwater pumping. Aravaipa Canyon contains one of the last pristine streams in the state.

Some of the common deciduous trees you'll find here are Fremont cottonwood, Arizona ash, Arizona sycamore, and Arizona black walnut. Saguaro cacti are found on the hillsides above the canyon bottom, and during the spring after a wet winter, the desert hills are carpeted with wildflowers.

Wildlife includes mule deer, white-tailed deer, javelina, bobcats, desert bighorn sheep, and mountain lions. And Aravaipa Canyon is famous among bird-watchers for the large number of species that take advantage of the easy living.

65. Powers Garden

RATING	🚶 🚶 🚶 🚶
DISTANCE	15.6 miles round-trip
HIKING TIME	2 days
ELEVATION GAIN	1,630 feet
HIGH POINT	6,512 feet
EFFORT	Prepare to Perspire
BEST SEASON	Spring, fall
WATER	Seasonal at Deer Creek Spring, Mud Spring, and Powers Garden Spring
PERMITS/CONTACT	None/Coronado National Forest, (520) 388-8300, www.fs.usda.gov/coronado
MAPS	USGS Kennedy Peak
NOTES	Leashed dogs welcome. Many of the trails shown on the topo maps are no longer present.

THE HIKE

This hike takes you into the heart of the seldom-visited Galiuro Wilderness. The Deer Creek Trail is probably the most popular, but even it is not crowded. The trail takes you to the remains of the historic Powers Garden ranch.

GETTING THERE

From Safford, drive 15 miles west on U.S. 70 and turn left on Klondyke Road. Drive 24.5 miles and turn left on Aravaipa Road. Continue 4.6 miles, then turn right on Forest Road 253 and continue 7.4 miles to the Deer Creek trailhead. The access roads are dirt and may be impassable during winter or wet weather. Elevation 3,368 feet, GPS coordinates N34°01.884'; W111°22.215'

THE TRAIL

Follow the Deer Creek Trail southwest up the head of Deer Creek past Deer Creek Cabin and then up a broad switchback over a pass. The trail heads west and drops down to cross Oak Creek, then climbs across a hillside through pinyon-juniper woodland to pass Mud Spring. The trail continues generally west, climbing around the heads of several tributaries

One of the least visited of the sky island ranges, the Galiuro Mountains are the place for solitude.

of Oak Creek. After swinging around the end of a ridge, the trail crosses the heads of several tributaries of Sycamore Creek before reaching the high point of the hike at Topout Divide, 5.1 miles, a pass between Topout Peak and Rockhouse Peak.

Follow the Deer Creek Trail west and northwest down Horse Canyon to Rattlesnake Canyon at 7.5 miles. Turn left on the Powers Garden Trail

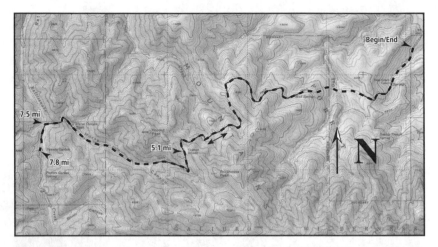

and hike 0.3 mile south to a broad meadow and the old Powers Garden ranch house. A seasonal spring in the drainage just north of the ranch house usually has water, and there are plenty of campsites under tall ponderosa pines in the area.

The Powers family established the ranch at Powers Garden in the remote upper reaches of Rattlesnake Canyon around 1900. To support themselves they farmed small plots in the canyon bottom and also operated several mines. In 1918, three of the Powerses became involved in a gunfight with lawmen who were trying to arrest the two Powers brothers as draft dodgers. Their father was killed, but the two brothers along with a friend escaped and became the subject of a massive manhunt. This gunfight took place at a cabin on a mining claim 5.0 miles south of Powers Garden, and bullet holes are still visible in the walls of the cabin.

GOING FARTHER
There are miles of trails shown on the topo maps of the Galiuro Wilderness, but many of these trails are overgrown and no longer passable.

66. Cochise Stronghold East

RATING	🚶 🚶 🚶 🚶
DISTANCE	5.5 miles round-trip
HIKING TIME	4 hours
ELEVATION GAIN	1,040 feet
HIGH POINT	5,960 feet
EFFORT	Moderate Workout
BEST SEASON	Year-round
WATER	Seasonal at Cochise Spring
PERMITS/CONTACT	None/Coronado National Forest, (520) 388-8300, www.fs.usda.gov/coronado
MAPS	USGS Cochise Stronghold
NOTES	Leashed dogs welcome

THE HIKE

A hike to a pass in the heart of Cochise Stronghold, this walk features views of the rugged granite formations of the Dragoon Mountains.

GETTING THERE

From Willcox, drive 9.6 miles west on Interstate 10 and turn left on U.S. 191. Drive 17.5 miles south on U.S. 191 and turn right on Ironwood Road. Continue west 9 miles to the end of the road at Cochise Stronghold Campground. The access roads are dirt and may be impassable during winter or wet weather. Elevation 4,923 feet, GPS coordinates N31°55.318'; W109°58.052'

THE TRAIL

From the trailhead, follow the Cochise Stronghold Trail southeast into Stronghold Canyon, where it turns south and heads up the canyon. After passing Cochise Spring at mile 0.9, the trail climbs into a basin and then turns northwest. After passing Halfmoon Tank, an old rancher's stock tank, the trail climbs over a low saddle and then makes a final ascent to a saddle on the main crest of the Dragoon Mountains. This scenic spot overlooking the rugged granite terrain of the Dragoons is the turnaround point for the hike at mile 2.75.

Desert bighorn sheep prefer steep, rocky mountainsides where they can watch for predators from above.

Cochise was a leader of the Chiricahua Apache. From 1850 until 1861 a tenuous peace was maintained, but then a U.S. Army officer invited Cochise to an army encampment and then accused Cochise of a raid on a local ranch. Cochise was innocent and offered to help find the responsible Apache, but when Lt. Bascom attempted to arrest him Cochise escaped. Cochise led his warriors on many raids against the encroaching white settlers from 1861 until 1872. During the American Civil War, the U.S. Army withdrew from the Arizona Territory and Apache raiders had free rein. After the war ended, the settlers demanded protection and the army renewed its attempts to pacify the Apache. Toward the end Cochise and his followers retreated to the rugged Dragoon Mountains where they eluded capture until a peace treaty was signed in 1872.

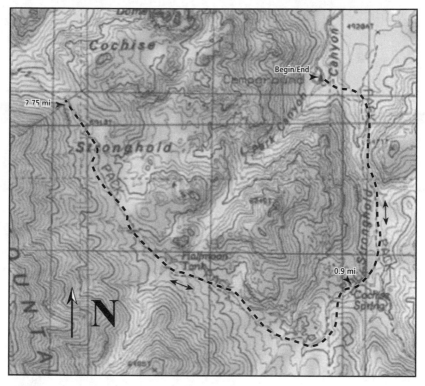

GOING FARTHER

The trail continues over the saddle and down into Stronghold Canyon West to end after 1.3 miles. If you do this, remember you will have an 800-foot climb back up to the saddle, so plan accordingly.

67. Sugarloaf Mountain

RATING	🚶 🚶 🚶 🚶
DISTANCE	1.7 miles round-trip
HIKING TIME	2 hours
ELEVATION GAIN	500 feet
HIGH POINT	7,310 feet
EFFORT	Easy Walk
BEST SEASON	Year-round
WATER	None
PERMITS/CONTACT	Entrance fee/Chiricahua National Monument, (520) 824-3560, www.nps.gov/chir
MAPS	USGS Cochise Head
NOTES	Dogs prohibited on trails in the national monument

THE HIKE

This easy walk takes you to a high point with a great view of the weird hoodoo rock formations of the northern Chiricahua Mountains.

GETTING THERE

From Willcox on Interstate 10, drive 31.3 miles east on AZ 186 and turn left on AZ 181. Continue 3 miles and turn left on Bonita Canyon Drive. Drive 2.1 miles to Chiricahua National Monument Visitor Center and continue another 4.9 miles to the Sugarloaf Mountain turnoff. Turn right

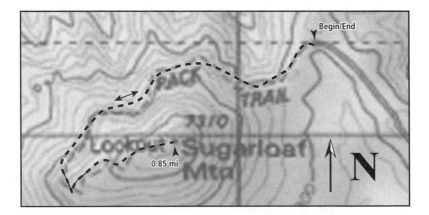

Rhyolite Canyon cuts a deep swath into the northern Chiricahua Mountains.

and drive 0.6 mile to a picnic area and the trailhead. Elevation 6,820 feet, GPS coordinates N32°00.992'; W109°19.246'

THE TRAIL

Initially, the trail heads southwest up a shallow ridge, but then climbs across the north slopes of the small mountain. A single switchback takes the trail up the west ridge of the mountain to the fire lookout on its summit. The tower is staffed during the summer fire season—ask permission of the lookout before climbing the stairs.

68. Echo Canyon

RATING	🚶 🚶 🚶 🚶 🚶
DISTANCE	2.7-mile loop
HIKING TIME	2 hours
ELEVATION GAIN	550 feet
HIGH POINT	6,770 feet
EFFORT	Easy Walk
BEST SEASON	Year-round
WATER	None
PERMITS/CONTACT	None/Chiricahua National Monument, (520) 824-3560, www.nps.gov/chir
MAPS	USGS Cochise Head; Chiricahua National Monument brochure map
NOTES	Dogs prohibited on trails in the national monument

THE HIKE

The classic loop through the volcanic hoodoos of Chiricahua National Monument, the hike threads through narrow passages between impressive stone towers.

The Echo Canyon Trail loops through the hoodoos of Echo and Rhyolite Canyons.

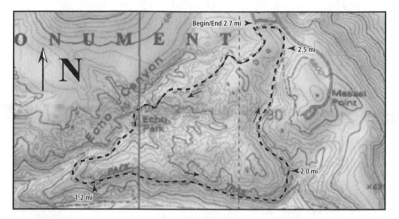

GETTING THERE
From Willcox on Interstate 10, drive 31.3 miles east on AZ 186 and turn left on AZ 181. Continue 3 miles and turn left on Bonita Canyon Drive. Drive 2.1 miles to Chiricahua National Monument Visitor Center and continue another 5.1 miles to the Echo Canyon trailhead. Elevation 6,788 feet, GPS coordinates N32°00.720'; W109°18.944'

THE TRAIL
From the Echo Canyon parking area, stay right on the Echo Canyon Trail and follow it southwest as it works its way between rock formations. The trail briefly drops into the bed of Echo Canyon at Echo Park before climbing out the south side and contouring around into upper Rhyolite Canyon.

At **1.2** miles, the Echo Canyon Trail ends at a junction; stay left on the Hailstone Trail and follow it east along the north slopes of Rhyolite Canyon. In complete contrast to the confined passages of Echo Canyon, the open slopes have great views of the hundreds of stone hoodoos across Rhyolite Canyon.

At another trail junction at **2.0** miles, turn left on the Ed Riggs Trail and follow it north up a tributary canyon. Stay left at **2.5** miles, where the Massai Point Trail comes in from the right, and hike 0.2 mile back to the Echo Canyon parking area.

GOING FARTHER
You can make this into a long loop hike by returning on the Big Balanced Rock and Mushroom Trails. Heart of Rocks (hike #69 in this guide) offers yet another way of reaching this area.

69. Heart of Rocks

RATING	🚶 🚶 🚶 🚶 🚶
DISTANCE	6.4 miles round-trip
HIKING TIME	8 hours
ELEVATION GAIN	1,450 feet
HIGH POINT	6,840 feet
EFFORT	Prepare to Perspire
BEST SEASON	Spring, fall
WATER	None
PERMITS/CONTACT	None/Chiricahua National Monument, (520) 824-3560, www.nps.gov/chir
MAPS	USGS Cochise Head, Rustler Park
NOTES	Dogs prohibited on trails in the national monument

THE HIKE

This longer hikes gets you away from the crowds and into one of the finest stone hoodoo areas of the national monument.

GETTING THERE

From Willcox on Interstate 10, drive 31.3 miles east on AZ 186 and turn left on AZ 181. Continue 3 miles and turn left on Bonita Canyon Drive. Drive 2.1 miles to Chiricahua National Monument Visitor Center and the trailhead. Elevation 5,381 feet, GPS coordinates N32°00.327'; W109°21.393'

THE TRAIL

Hike east up Rhyolite Canyon on the Lower Rhyolite Canyon Trail, which follows the bed of the canyon through a mix of pinyon-juniper woodland and chaparral brush. At **1.5 miles**, turn right on the Sara Deming Trail and follow it southeast up Sara Deming Canyon. The shadier recesses of this canyon feature tall ponderosa pine and slightly shorter Apache pine. The trail climbs out of the canyon to the north and meets the Big Balanced Rock Trail at **2.8 miles**.

Turn left on the Heart of Rocks Trail. At **2.9 miles** you'll reach a T intersection. Turn left to hike the 0.6-mile but intricate Heart of Rocks

Pinnacle Balanced Rock is only one of many weird rock formations along the Heart of Rocks loop.

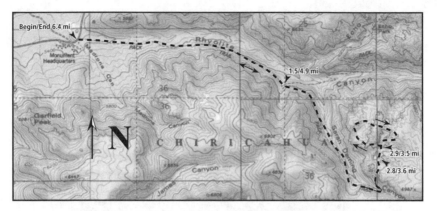

Loop. You'll return to this same junction at **3.5** miles; turn left to retrace your steps and return to the visitor center trailhead.

GOING FARTHER

You can make a longer loop hike from the junction with the Big Balanced Rock Trail by heading east on that trail, which almost immediately passes its namesake rock. After 1 mile, a 0.5-mile side trail leads out to Inspiration Point, a side hike well worth taking. From the trail junction, continue east on the Mushroom Rock Trail, which soon drops into Hunt Canyon and turns north. After 1.2 miles turn left on the Hailstone Trail and follow it 0.8 mile west down Rhyolite Canyon to the Upper Rhyolite Canyon/Echo Canyon junction. Turn left and follow the Upper Rhyolite Canyon Trail east down a switchback and then west down into Rhyolite Canyon 1.1 miles to the Sara Deming Trail junction. Stay left on the Lower Rhyolite Canyon Trail and follow it 1.5 miles back to the trailhead at the visitor center.

70. Buena Vista Peak

RATING	𝿖 𝿖 𝿖 𝿖
DISTANCE	2.0 miles round-trip
HIKING TIME	1 hour
ELEVATION GAIN	300 feet
HIGH POINT	8,720 feet
EFFORT	Easy Walk
BEST SEASON	Spring–fall
WATER	None
PERMITS/CONTACT	None/Coronado National Forest, (520) 388-8300, www.fs.usda.gov/coronado
MAPS	USGS Rustler Park
NOTES	Leashed dogs welcome

THE HIKE

This nice little hike takes you to the top of Buena Vista Peak, which means "good view" in Spanish. And it is truly a good view, looking over the north end of the high Chiricahua Mountains.

GETTING THERE

From Willcox on Interstate 10, drive 34 miles east on AZ 186, then turn left on AZ 181. Continue 3 miles and then turn right on Pinery Canyon Road (Forest Road 42). Drive 12 miles to Onion Saddle and turn right on Rustler Park Road (FR 42D). Drive 2.8 miles to Rustler Park trailhead. The access roads are dirt and may be impassable during winter or wet weather. Elevation 8,393 feet, GPS coordinates N31°54.374'; W109°16.689'

THE TRAIL

From the trailhead, walk west on the Crest Trail, which climbs onto the ridge west of the campground. After just 0.1 mile, turn right on the Buena Vista Peak Trail and follow it north up the ridge to the fire lookout structure on the summit.

The lookout building, apparently no longer in use, was sometimes staffed during high fire danger. The Coronado National Forest no longer uses many of its lookouts, but other national forests, including the

Barfoot Peak as seen from the rocky summit of Buena Vista Peak.

Coconino and Kaibab in northern Arizona, and the Apache-Sitgreaves in eastern Arizona, still find lookouts a cost-effective way of maintaining a continuous fire watch. When the lookout spots smoke and verifies, usually with the aid of binoculars, that it is not a plume of dust or something else, he or she uses an Osborne Firefinder to precisely measure the bearing to the fire. The lookout then calls in the bearing along with observations on the behavior of the fire to the forest dispatcher. If other lookouts can see the fire, the dispatcher triangulates the multiple bearings to locate the fire on a map. The dispatcher may then dispatch a recon airplane to have a close look, a helitack crew (helicopter-borne firefighters), and fire engines and hand crews. The value of lookouts lies in early detection,

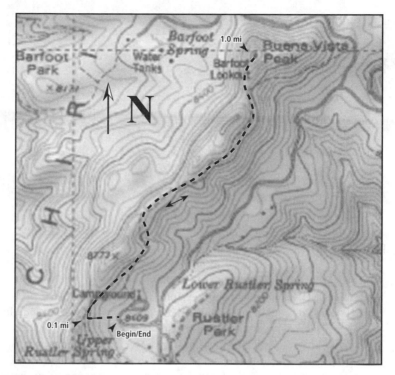

which often allows crews to contain wildfires while they are small—a far easier and safer task than stopping a huge crown fire.

GOING FARTHER

A large network of trails covers the high Chiricahuas and provides many opportunities for day hikes and backpack trips. (See hike #71 in this guide.)

71. Chiricahua Peak

RATING	𝄪 𝄪 𝄪 𝄪 𝄪
DISTANCE	10.2 miles round-trip
HIKING TIME	7 hours
ELEVATION GAIN	1,350 feet
HIGH POINT	9,759 feet
EFFORT	Moderate Workout
BEST SEASON	Summer, fall
WATER	Seasonal at Tub Spring, Booger Spring, and Anita Spring
PERMITS/CONTACT	None/Coronado National Forest, (520) 388-8300, www.fs.usda.gov/coronado
MAPS	USGS Rustler Park, Chiricahua Peak
NOTES	Leashed dogs welcome. The entire Chiricahua Mountains burned in the 222,954-acre Horseshoe Two wildfire during the summer of 2011. While not all the forest was destroyed, you can expect variable conditions as well as deadfall along the trail. Check with the Forest Service for the latest conditions before planning your hike.

THE HIKE

This hike along the beautiful crest of the Chiricahua Mountains ends at Chiricahua Peak, the highest summit in this sky island range at 9,759 feet. Once covered by a nearly unbroken mixed forest of ponderosa and Apache pine, Douglas fir, white fir, blue spruce, and quaking aspen, this area has been turned into a mosaic of burned and unburned forest. by repeated wildfires.

GETTING THERE

From Willcox on Interstate 10, drive 34 miles east on AZ 186, then turn left on AZ 181. Continue 3 miles and then turn right on Pinery Canyon Road (Forest Road 42). Drive 12 miles to Onion Saddle and turn right on Rustler Park Road (FR 42D). Drive 2.8 miles to Rustler Park trailhead. The access roads are dirt and may be impassable during winter or wet weather. Elevation 8,393 feet, GPS coordinates N31°54.374'; W109°16.689'

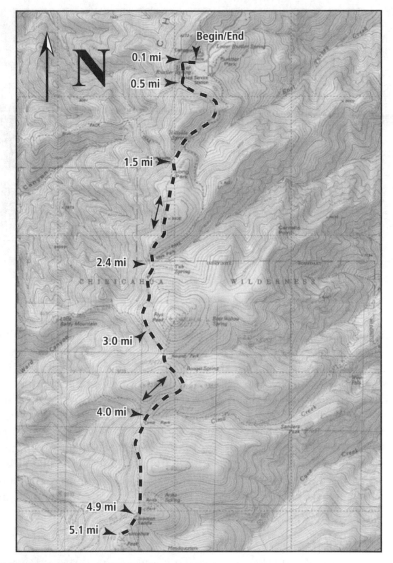

THE TRAIL

Hike west **0.1** mile from the trailhead and then turn left and hike south on the Crest Trail. At **0.5** mile a trail comes in from the right; continue straight ahead on the Crest Trail. The trail contours around the east side of a hill and comes into Bootlegger Saddle at **1.5** miles, where there is another trail junction; again, stay left on the Crest Trail. Now, the Crest

Monte Vista Peak is a great side hike from Chiricahua Peak.

Trail climbs over an unnamed hill and descends to Flys Park in another saddle at **2.4** miles. Tub Spring is located to the east at the end of a short spur trail. Continue south on the crest trail as it contours around the west side of Flys Peak. The Salisbury Trail comes in from the right at **3.0** miles. Continue south on the Crest Trail to Round Park, another meadow located in a saddle. A spur trail goes left to Booger Spring. Now, the Crest Trail contours around the east side of a hill and into the saddle at Cima Park, **4.0** miles. The Cima Creek Trail goes left, but once again continue straight ahead and hike south to Anita Park and Junction Saddle at **4.9** miles. A spur trail goes left to Anita Spring. Trails contour around both the west and east sides of Chiricahua Peak—head straight up the ridge on a short trail to the rounded summit.

GOING FARTHER
A nice extension of this hike takes you 2.6 miles south on the Crest Trail to the top of Monte Vista Peak, a bald summit with a much better view than Chiricahua Peak.

72. Rucker Canyon

RATING	🚶 🚶 🚶 🚶
DISTANCE	5.7 miles round trip
HIKING TIME	4 hours
ELEVATION GAIN	520 feet
HIGH POINT	6,630 feet
EFFORT	Easy Walk
BEST SEASON	Spring–fall
WATER	Rucker Creek
PERMITS/CONTACT	None/Coronado National Forest, (520) 388-8300, www.fs.usda.gov/coronado
MAPS	USGS Chiricahua Peak
NOTES	Leashed dogs welcome. The entire Chiricahua Mountains burned in the 222,954-acre Horseshoe Two wildfire during the summer of 2011. While not all the forest was destroyed, you can expect variable conditions as well as deadfall along the trail. Check with the Forest Service for the latest conditions before planning your hike.

THE HIKE

This is an easy and pleasant walk along a mountain stream in the southern Chiricahua Mountains.

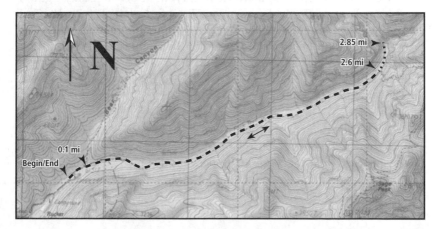

Rucker Creek tumbles through a forested canyon at the southern end of the Chiricahua Mountains.

GETTING THERE

From Douglas, drive 31.3 miles north on U.S. 191 and turn right on Rucker Canyon Road. Drive 14.9 miles and turn left to remain on Rucker Canyon Road. Continue 6.9 miles, then turn left on Forest Road 74E. Drive 5.5 miles to the end of the road at Rucker Campground and trailhead. The access roads are dirt and may be impassable during winter or wet weather. Elevation 6,110 feet, GPS coordinates N31°47.019'; W109°18.275'

THE TRAIL

Follow the Rucker Trail east up Rucker Canyon; at **0.1** mile stay right on the Rucker Trail where the Bear Canyon Trail forks left. The Rucker Trail crosses the creek several times as it makes its way up the forested canyon floor. At **2.6** miles the Rucker Trail leaves the streamside and climbs out of the canyon to the southeast. For a glimpse of the wilderness canyon, hike 2.5 miles cross-country up the canyon to the point where the canyon narrows and turns north.

GOING FARTHER

The Rucker Trail connects with the extensive trail system in the Chiricahua Wilderness, and there are many possibilities for extended day hikes and backpack trips.

73. Mount Wrightson

RATING	🚶 🚶 🚶 🚶 🚶
DISTANCE	11.6 miles round-trip
HIKING TIME	8 hours
ELEVATION GAIN	4,020 feet
HIGH POINT	9,453 feet
EFFORT	Knee-Punishing
BEST SEASON	Summer, fall
WATER	Sprung Spring, Baldy Spring, Bellows Spring
PERMITS/CONTACT	None/Coronado National Forest, (520) 388-8300, www.fs.usda.gov/coronado
MAPS	USGS Mount Wrightson
NOTES	Leashed dogs welcome

THE HIKE

This hike to the summit of the Santa Rita Mountains uses the aptly named Super Trail for the ascent, and a portion of the shorter Old Baldy Trail for the return.

GETTING THERE

From Tucson, drive about 25 miles south on Interstate 19 and exit at Continental. Drive east through Continental and continue 13.9 miles on Madera Canyon Road to Roundup trailhead at the end of the road. Elevation 5,436 feet, GPS coordinates N31°42.811'; W110°52.403'

THE TRAIL

Start on the Super Trail, which climbs away from the trailhead at a steady grade via a couple of switchbacks, then drops into Madera Creek. After following the creek for a short distance, the trail switchbacks to the north, rounds the end of a brushy ridge, then heads south along the east slopes of upper Madera Canyon. After passing Sprung Spring, the trail reaches a multiple trail junction at Josephine Saddle. Turn left to stay on the Super Trail.

At **3.4** miles, the Old Baldy Trail comes in from the left; this will be your return trail. Stay right and follow the Super Trail south. After a broad switchback, the trail continues around the south slopes of Mount

Madera Canyon is a world-class birding area, partly because Madera Creek provides an oasis in the surrounding desert.

Wrightson, passing through Riley Saddle. The Gardner Trail goes right at 5.4 miles; stay left on the Super Trail and continue around the northeast slopes of Mount Wrightson.

Soon after the Super Trail passes Baldy Spring, it arrives at Baldy Saddle on the main crest of the range and a four-way trail junction at 6.1 miles. Turn sharply left on the Old Baldy Trail, which heads south

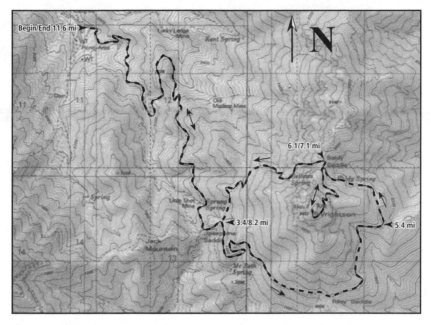

toward the rocky summit of Mount Wrightson. The trail works its way up the northeast side of the mountain to the summit at **6.6** miles.

After enjoying the expansive view of southern Arizona and northern Sonora, retrace your steps 0.5 mile to Baldy Saddle. Turn left on the Old Baldy Trail, which starts a steep descent to the east and passes Bellows Spring. The trail heads down the northwest slopes of the mountain and meets the Super Trail at **8.2** miles, which closes the loop portion of the hike. Turn right and follow the Super Trail back to the Roundup trailhead.

Madera Canyon is a birder's paradise. Since the Santa Ritas are so close to Mexico, several Mexican species, such as the colorful Elegant Trogon, are commonly found here.

GOING FARTHER

Mount Wrightson can be climbed via several other trails, all of which are longer and steeper than the Super Trail. If you have time, a nice side hike starts from Baldy Saddle. Head north on the Crest Trail about 0.5 mile for views of the east side of the wilderness.

74. Sycamore Creek

RATING	🚶 🚶 🚶 🚶
DISTANCE	11.2 miles round-trip
HIKING TIME	6 hours
ELEVATION GAIN	515 feet
HIGH POINT	4,000 feet
EFFORT	Moderate Workout
BEST SEASON	Spring, fall
WATER	Sycamore Creek
PERMITS/CONTACT	None/Coronado National Forest, (520) 388-8300, www.fs.usda.gov/coronado
MAPS	USGS Ruby
NOTES	Leashed dogs welcome

THE HIKE

An easy cross-country walk, this hike follows Sycamore Creek through the Pajarita Wilderness to the Mexican border. Because of the perennial stream, Sycamore Creek is a major wildlife corridor and important bird habitat.

Arizona hikers are obsessed with water because it is so rare and precious in the desert.

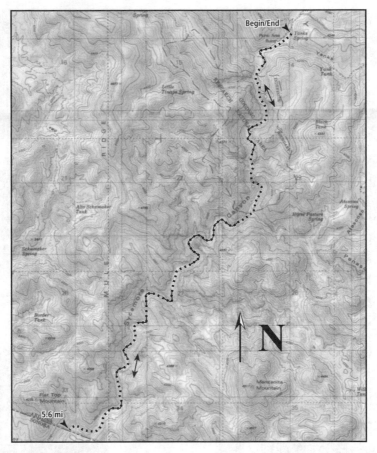

GETTING THERE

From Tucson, drive about 55 miles south on Interstate 19 and exit onto AZ 289. Go about 20 miles and turn left at the Sycamore Canyon sign. Drive 0.5 mile to the trailhead at Hank and Yank Spring. The access roads are dirt and may be impassible during winter or wet weather. Elevation 4,003 feet, GPS coordinates N31°25.820'; W111°11.398'

THE TRAIL

Although there is no trail, it is easy to follow the creek downstream. The lush streamside vegetation, Fremont cottonwoods, and Arizona sycamore trees provide a welcome green break from the desert. You can follow the canyon as far south as you want, but the mandatory turnaround point is the fence at the Mexican border, 5.6 miles.

Elusive gray foxes prefer rocky, brushy, and forested areas in Arizona.

WESTERN DESERTS

The southwestern third of Arizona is classic basin and range country with long, low mountain ranges isolated by broad desert plains. Although many of the ranges are now protected as wilderness areas, there are not as many hiking trails in this area as there are in other parts of the state. That is why the hikes in this section are scattered over a large area.

Several of the hikes lead to desert summits with extensive views, while others explore desert canyons. As long as you don't try to hike the lowest elevations during the summer heat, you'll find this desert region very enjoyable to explore during the fall, winter, and early spring.

WESTERN DESERTS

75. Cherum Peak Trail

RATING	🚶 🚶 🚶
DISTANCE	4.1 miles round-trip
HIKING TIME	3 hours
ELEVATION GAIN	1,032 feet
HIGH POINT	6,978 feet
EFFORT	Moderate Workout
BEST SEASON	Spring, fall
WATER	None
PERMITS/CONTACT	None/Bureau of Land Management, (928) 718-3700, www.blm.gov/az/st/en.html
MAPS	USGS Chloride
NOTES	Leashed dogs welcome

THE HIKE

This hike follows a trail to the top of Cherum Peak. Though not the highest point in the Cerbat Mountains, it is the only summit with a trail to the top. Two BLM campgrounds along the access road provide places to camp with a view, if you'd like to spend more time in the area.

GETTING THERE

From Kingman at the U.S. 93 exit from Interstate 40, drive 22.1 miles northwest on U.S. 93 and turn right on the Big Wash Road. Drive 12.5 miles to the signed Cherum Peak trailhead, on the left. The access roads are dirt and may be impassable during winter or wet weather. Elevation 5,998 feet, GPS coordinates N35°24.930'; W114°09.009'

The Cerbat and Hualapai Mountains as seen from Cherum Peak.

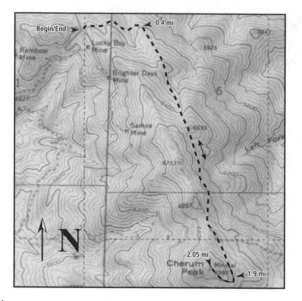

THE TRAIL

Follow the Cherum Peak Trail east as it descends slightly to cross two drainages before turning south at mile **0.4** and climbing up a ridge. The ascent continues through pinyon pine–juniper woodland as the trail climbs along the east slopes and gradually gets nearer to the crest. Finally, the trail makes a sharp turn to the northwest at mile **1.9** and climbs to the summit. The last few yards are a rock scramble.

From this 6,983-foot summit, your view spans the rugged pinnacles at the north end of the range to the 8,000-foot Hualapai Mountains to the south.

As you hike through the pinyon-juniper woodland, you'll almost certainly hear the distinct high, nasal, upwardly inflected call of the pinyon jay. One of the few birds able to live in the dry pinyon-juniper woodlands that cover much of the intermountain west at intermediate elevations, the pinyon jay not only survives, it thrives. A highly social bird often found in flocks of 500 or more, this large, dull blue member of the intelligent corvid family (which includes ravens and crows) lives primarily on pinyon pine nuts. These tasty and highly nutritious nuts are prized by humans and animals alike. Since individual pinyon pines only bear seeds about every five years, the pinyon jay harvests the seeds when they are available and hides them in caches for future use. The bird buries the seeds a few inches deep in the sandy soil. Tests have shown that pinyon jays can find about 90 percent of their caches, even when buried under a few inches of snow.

76. Wabayuma Peak

RATING	🚶 🚶 🚶
DISTANCE	5.4 miles round-trip
HIKING TIME	5 hours
ELEVATION GAIN	1,530 feet
HIGH POINT	7,601 feet
EFFORT	Prepare to Perspire
BEST SEASON	Spring–fall
WATER	None
PERMITS/CONTACT	None/Bureau of Land Management, (928) 718-3700, www.blm.gov/az/st/en.html
MAPS	USGS Wabayuma Peak
NOTES	Leashed dogs welcome. The last 0.8 mile is a steep cross-country hike.

THE HIKE

If you want to escape the crowds, this is your hike. Unlike the northern end of the Hualapai Mountains, which serve as the main escape from summer heat for the residents of Kingman, the Wabayuma Peak area sees very few visitors, yet is a beautiful spread of shear granite outcrops, pinyon-juniper woodland, and the occasional tall ponderosa pine.

GETTING THERE

From Kingman on AZ 66, go south on Hualapai Mountain Road past Hualapai Mountain Park. Continue past Wild Cow Campground to Waba-yuma Peak trailhead, 28.9 miles south of Kingman. The access roads are dirt and may be impassable during winter or wet weather. A high-clearance vehicle may be required. Elevation 6,066 feet, GPS coordinates N34°57.209'; W113°54.943'

THE TRAIL

The trail starts out as an old jeep road and climbs northwest up a ridge through dense chaparral brush. After passing through a saddle at **0.9** miles the old road turns more to the west and continues to work its way up the main ridge crest. At **1.9** miles the old road drops down to another saddle, and turns away to the northeast. Leave the trail and climb northwest directly

Striking granite formations mark the summit of Wabayuma Peak, the highest point in the southern Hualapai Mountains.

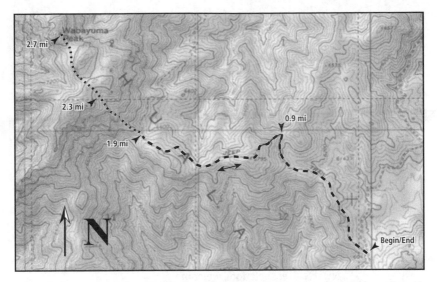

toward the crest of the mountains. You may find traces of an informal trail. Once on the crest at a broad saddle at 2.3 miles, continue northwest across gentler terrain and work your way through the granite outcrops. Pass around the west side of a rocky hill, cross another saddle, and scramble up to the rocky summit of Wabayuma Peak.

Chaparral brush as encountered on this hike and many others in Arizona is not a single plant but rather a mix of several brushy plants. The most common components are shrub live oak, mountain mahogany, and manzanita. Manzanita can be readily identified by its glossy red bark. All three are tough evergreen plants that grow together to form dense brush that averages about 3 to 4 feet high but can reach 6 feet. Although difficult to hike through, chaparral provides important cover and habitat for wildlife. Periodic wildfires are normal in chaparral, which usually burns intensely, leaving little but ash and stumps behind. Recovery is surprisingly rapid as the plants quickly grow from their roots after a fire. In five or ten years the slopes are again covered by dense brush.

77. Vulture Peak

RATING	🚶 🚶 🚶 🚶
DISTANCE	3.5 miles round-trip
HIKING TIME	5 hours
ELEVATION GAIN	1,160 feet
HIGH POINT	3,660 feet
EFFORT	Moderate Workout
BEST SEASON	Fall–spring
WATER	None
PERMITS/CONTACT	None/Bureau of Land Management, (623) 580-5500, www.blm.gov/az/st/en.html
MAPS	USGS Vulture Peak
NOTES	Leashed dogs welcome

THE HIKE
A scenic hike across open desert, the last portion requires a scramble to reach the rocky summit.

GETTING THERE
From U.S. 60 in Wickenburg, drive south 7 miles on the Vulture Mine Road. About 0.7 mile past milepost 30, turn left on the signed Vulture Peak Trail Road. Drive 0.4 mile to the trailhead. The access roads are dirt and may be impassable during winter or wet weather. Elevation 2,500 feet, GPS coordinates N33°52.664'; W112°49.095'

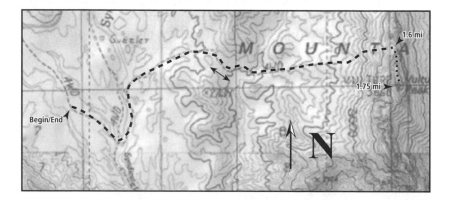

The moon looms in the sky over Vulture Peak.

THE TRAIL

Follow the Vulture Peak Trail southeast from the trailhead across a desert flat and Syndicate Wash. The trail heads north up the wash a short distance, then leaves the wash and travels east toward Vulture Peak. After passing through a broad saddle, the trail heads directly for a point on the main ridge just north of Vulture Peak, which it reaches at **1.6** miles. Turn right and scramble 0.2 mile south to the summit.

78. Ben Avery Trail

RATING	🚶 🚶 🚶 🚶
DISTANCE	7.8 miles round-trip
HIKING TIME	4 hours
ELEVATION GAIN	310 feet
HIGH POINT	1,850 feet
EFFORT	Moderate Workout
BEST SEASON	Fall–spring
WATER	Seasonal at Indian Spring
PERMITS/CONTACT	None/Bureau of Land Management, (928) 317-3200, www.blm.gov/az/st/en.html
MAPS	USGS Eagletail Mountains East, Eagletail Mountains West
NOTES	Leashed dogs welcome

THE HIKE

This hike in the Eagletail Mountains Wilderness leads past the blocky mass of Courthouse Rock deep into the heart of the rugged Eagletail Mountains.

GETTING THERE

Drive about 13 miles west of Tonopah on Interstate 10 and take Exit 81 for the Harquahala Valley, then drive south 5 miles to Courthouse Rock Road and turn right. Drive west 5 miles and turn right at a major fork onto a gas pipeline maintenance road. Drive 6 miles to a marked road going south. Follow this track 1.5 miles to the Ben Avery trailhead at the wilderness boundary. The access roads are dirt and may be impassable during winter or wet weather. Elevation 1,539 feet, GPS coordinates N33°28.849'; W113°21.553'

THE TRAIL

From the wilderness boundary and trailhead, walk southwest on the trail, which follows an old jeep trail past the northeast side of Courthouse Rock at 1.1 miles. The trail continues up a wash, turns west, and passes through a broad pass on the crest of the Eagletail Mountains at 2.4 miles. This is the high point of the hike. Turning again to the southwest, the trail descends a series of drainages to arrive at Indian Spring in a small canyon.

The 600-foot east face of Courthouse Rock, an isolated rock formation along the Ben Avery Trail.

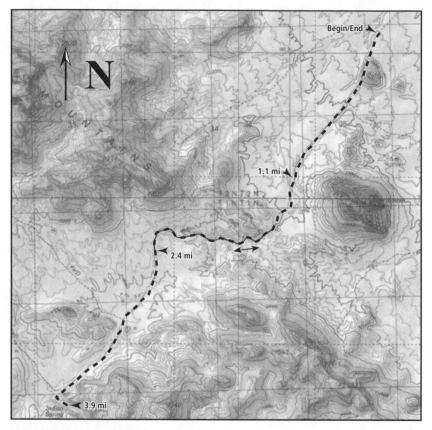

GOING FARTHER

The open terrain of the Eagletail Mountain foothills invites further exploration by hiking cross-country. Make sure you have the topo maps and a compass before setting off away from the trail.

79. Palm Canyon

RATING	𝄂 𝄂 𝄂
DISTANCE	1.1 miles round-trip
HIKING TIME	1 hour
ELEVATION GAIN	360 feet
HIGH POINT	2,480 feet
EFFORT	Easy Walk
BEST SEASON	Fall–spring
WATER	None
PERMITS/CONTACT	None/Kofa National Wildlife Refuge, (928) 783-7861, www.fws.gov/southwest/refuges/arizona/kofa/index.html
MAPS	USGS Palm Canyon
NOTES	Dogs prohibited in the national wildlife refuge. Do not leave pets in a car on warm or hot days.

THE HIKE

This short, easy hike leads to a unique stand of California fan palms, which are fairly common in the southeast deserts of California but very rare in Arizona.

GETTING THERE

From Quartzite, drive 18 miles south on AZ 95 and turn left onto Palm Canyon Road. Drive east 9 miles to the trailhead. The access roads are dirt and may be impassable during winter or wet weather. Elevation 2,117 feet, GPS coordinates N33°21.614'; W114°06.412'

THE TRAIL

Follow the trail 0.55 mile east up Palm Canyon to a viewpoint overlooking the palm trees. The grove is in a steep ravine on the north side of the canyon.

California fan palms grow in protected areas where there is some groundwater available. In the Palm Springs and Joshua Tree areas in California, the palms are often associated with springs, forming a palm oasis. Here in Palm Canyon, surface water rarely appears.

Because palm trees do not have annual growth rings, it is nearly impossible to date them. One theory holds that palms were more widespread

California fan palms only grow in sheltered recesses in the Kofa Mountains.

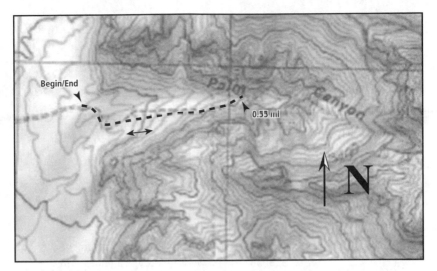

during the cooler, wetter climate of the last glacial period, but then became isolated to small stands as the climate warmed and dried. Other research suggests that birds or animals carry the seeds to establish new isolated groves.

As the palm fronds die, they droop downward to form a fringe around the trunk of the tree. Eventually the fronds fall off and provide ground cover, which helps young palms germinate. The dry fronds are extremely flammable and palm groves occasionally burn in wildfires. Fortunately the palms are surprisingly fire-resistant and usually survive.

GOING FARTHER

The Kofa National Wildlife Refuge was established in 1939 primarily to protect desert bighorn sheep. Although there is no trail system in the Kofa Mountains, the open desert terrain is relatively easy to explore by hiking cross-country. There are no permanent water sources, so it is most practical to day-hike rather than backpack. Be certain to bring not only plenty of water but also a topo map and compass.

80. Bull Pasture

RATING	🚶 🚶 🚶 🚶
DISTANCE	3.2 miles round-trip
HIKING TIME	2 hours
ELEVATION GAIN	1,010 feet
HIGH POINT	3,370 feet
EFFORT	Moderate Workout
BEST SEASON	Fall–spring
WATER	None. Bull Pasture Spring, shown on the topo map, is dry
PERMITS/CONTACT	None/Organ Pipe Cactus National Monument, (520) 387-6849, www.nps.gov/orpi/index.htm
MAPS	USGS Mount Ajo
NOTES	Dogs prohibited on trails in the national monument

THE HIKE

This scenic loop trail takes you into Bull Pasture, a desert basin at the foot of rugged Mount Ajo that was once used for grazing cattle.

GETTING THERE

From Ajo, drive 33 miles south to Organ Pipe Cactus National Monument Visitor Center and turn left on Ajo Mountain Loop Drive. Drive 8 miles to the signed Bull Pasture trailhead at the Estes Canyon Picnic Area. The access roads are dirt and may be impassable during winter or wet weather. Elevation 2,365 feet, GPS coordinates N32°00.945'; W112°42.710'

THE TRAIL

From the trailhead, follow the Bull Pasture Trail east up a small canyon. At the head of this canyon the trail climbs the slopes via a single switchback, then heads east again to meet the Estes Canyon Trail at **0.8** mile; this will be the return trail. Turn right to remain on the Bull Pasture Trail and follow it southeast up a steep ravine and then onto a rocky ridge. The trail ends at a viewpoint on this ridge at **1.3** miles. From this vantage point there is a nice view of the ramparts of Mount Ajo across the relatively gentle slopes of Bull Basin.

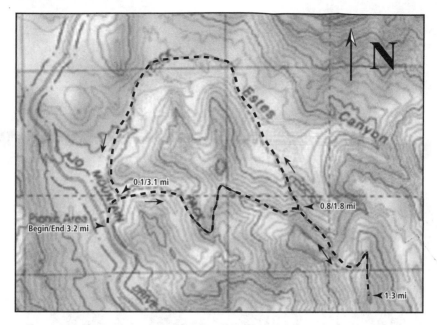

To return, retrace your steps to the Estes Trail junction at mile 1.8 and turn right on the Estes Canyon Trail. After the trail drops down the steep canyon slopes to the northwest, it follows the floor of Estes Canyon northwest and then south back to the trailhead, Watch for some fine examples of the monument's namesake cactus. Unlike saguaro cactus, organ pipe cactus produces many stems, which grow from a common basin. Though common in northern Sonora, organ pipe cactus is only found along the southern border of Arizona.

GOING FARTHER

It is possible to climb Mount Ajo from the end of the Bull Basin Trail, but be prepared for a rugged hike. Head east, cross-country, and work your way up to the main crest via slopes above Bull Pasture Spring. Be sure to note your descent point for the return, as the route down through the cliffs will not be obvious from above. Then walk north along the crest to the summit. This route is 3.4 miles round-trip, but you should allow at least four hours extra for the hike.

Organ pipe cactus resembles saguaro cactus but has many trunks rather than a single main stem.

Index

About the Author

Bruce Grubbs has been hiking, backpacking, and cross-country skiing throughout the American West for several decades. He participated in the technical first ascents of the last major summits to be climbed in the Grand Canyon. Bruce has spent more than 400 days hiking in the Grand Canyon. He continues to enjoy long backpacking treks through remote sections of the Grand Canyon, as well as hiking and backpacking trips elsewhere in the American West.

Outdoor writing and photography have always been part of Bruce's outdoor experiences. His first published article was in a local Arizona outdoor magazine, and he has since been published by *Backpacker Magazine* and several regional publications. Later, his writing focus expanded to include books, with the publication of *Hiking Arizona*, with Stewart Aitchison. He has since written more than 35 published books.

Earlier, Bruce worked 11 seasons as a wildland firefighter for the U.S. Forest Service and Bureau of Land Management. His positions included fire lookout, engine foreman, helitack foreman, and fire station manager.

He was part-owner of an outdoor shop for eight years. More recently, he started and continues to run a successful computer consulting business, offering personal computer support and website design to individual clients and small businesses.

Bruce has been a professional pilot for more than 25 years and has over 8,000 hours of flight time.

Other interests include amateur radio, where he served for several years as the local amateur radio emergency coordinator for Coconino County, Arizona. He also is a mountain biker, sea kayaker, and figure skater.